Wormleysburg

Jewel on the Susquehanna

by

Lawrence von Knorr
Tammi Knorr

Cover image: *Wormleysburg Shore at St. Paul's* by Lawrence von Knorr

Wormleysburg: Jewel on the Susquehanna

FIRST SUNBURY PRESS EDITION
Printed in the United States of America
October 2010

ISBN 978-1-934597-19-4

Published by:
Sunbury Press, Inc.
436 E Crestwood Dr
Camp Hill, PA 17011-1212

www.sunburypress.com

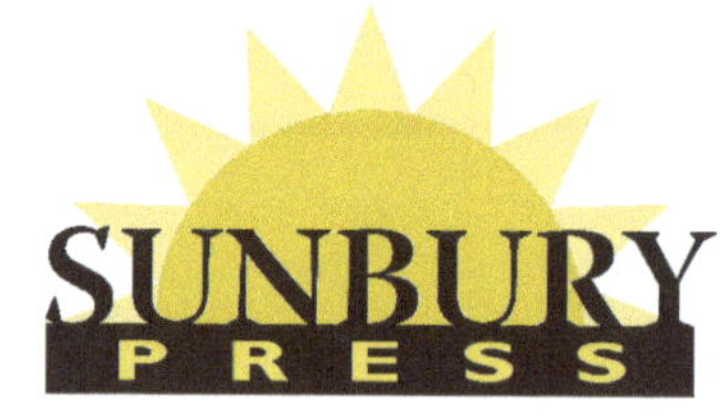

Camp Hill, Pennsylvania USA

"Here, on the river's verge, I could be busy for months without changing my place, simply leaning a little more to right or left."

Paul Cezanne (1839-1906)

Dedication

To our fellow 'Wormleysburgers' – may you see our little hometown in new ways.

Lawrence von Knorr
& Tammi Knorr

Introduction

Since moving to Wormleysburg, Pennsylvania in November, 2009, Lawrence and Tammi have grown to love their adopted hometown. In August of 2010 they opened the West Shore Gallery at 100 South Front Street in the borough. As of this writing, it is Wormleysburg's only fine art gallery and photography studio. During their many short trips to and from their home to the gallery, the couple began to appreciate more and more the natural and architectural beauty of the area, They decided to use their talent as photographers and digital artists to create this little time capsule of the town.

Contents

This book presents the photography of Tammi Knorr and the digital fine art of Lawrence von Knorr.

Tammi Knorr is known for her unusual compositions of 'everyday things', discovering odd angles and details in her surroundings. She is an accomplished wedding, portrait and commercial photographer. This is Tammi's first book.

Lawrence von Knorr is a pioneer in Photo Impressionism – using computer software to turn his photographs into painterly creations. Lawrence's award-winning work has been shown in major cities across the country.

Wormleysburg, for those who do not know, is the borough on the west shore of the Susquehanna River, directly across from Harrisburg in Cumberland County. Home to approximately 3,000 people, Wormleysburg is known for its riverside restaurants, railroad tracks and shoreline. It is a bedroom community with easy access to the city and water sports. The old town along the river was once a ferry crossing point and contains many early 19th century homes and buildings. Up on the hill, newer developments were built in the 1960's and later. It is also home for the headquarters of both Harsco Corporation and Rite Aid.

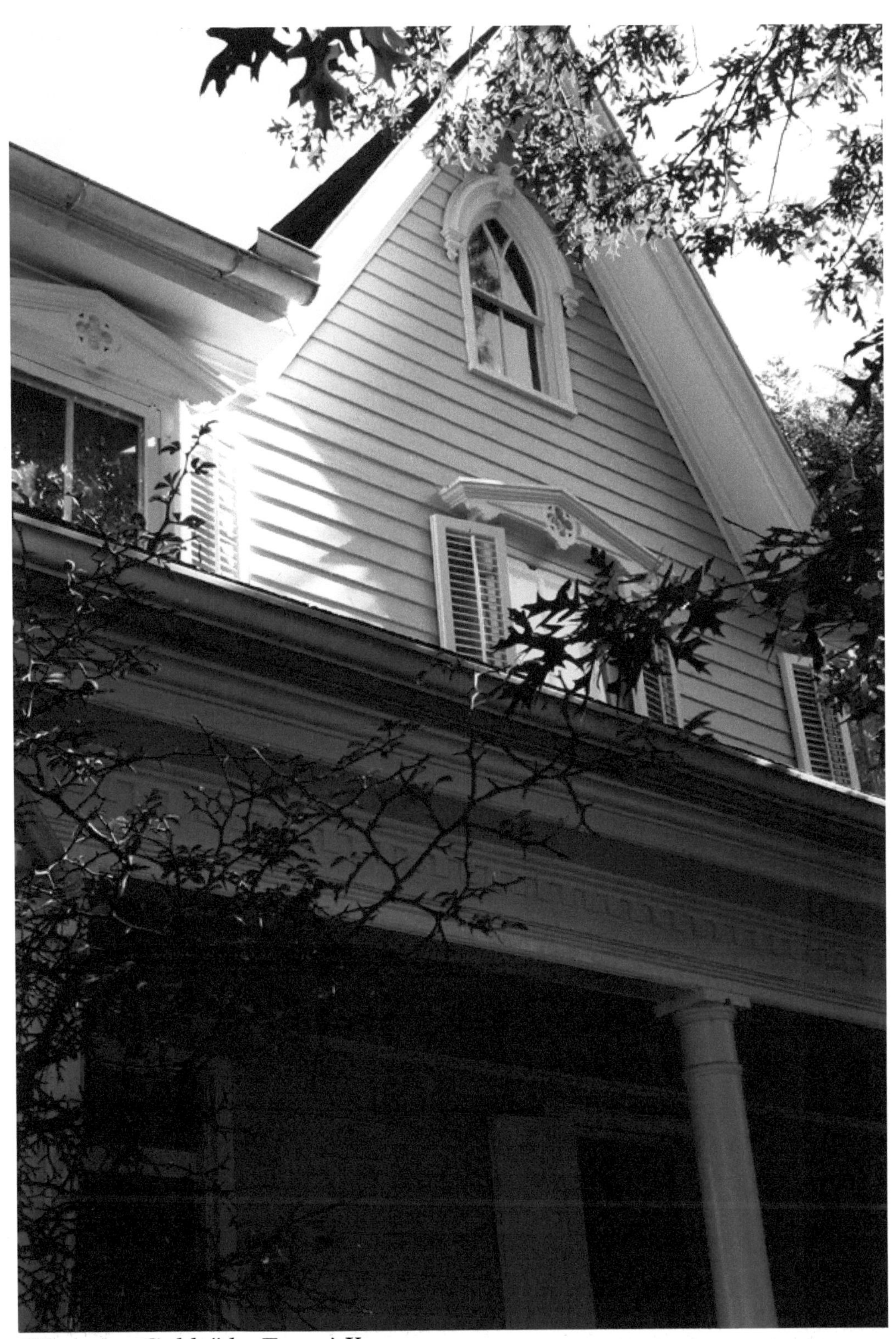

"Victorian Gable" by Tammi Knorr

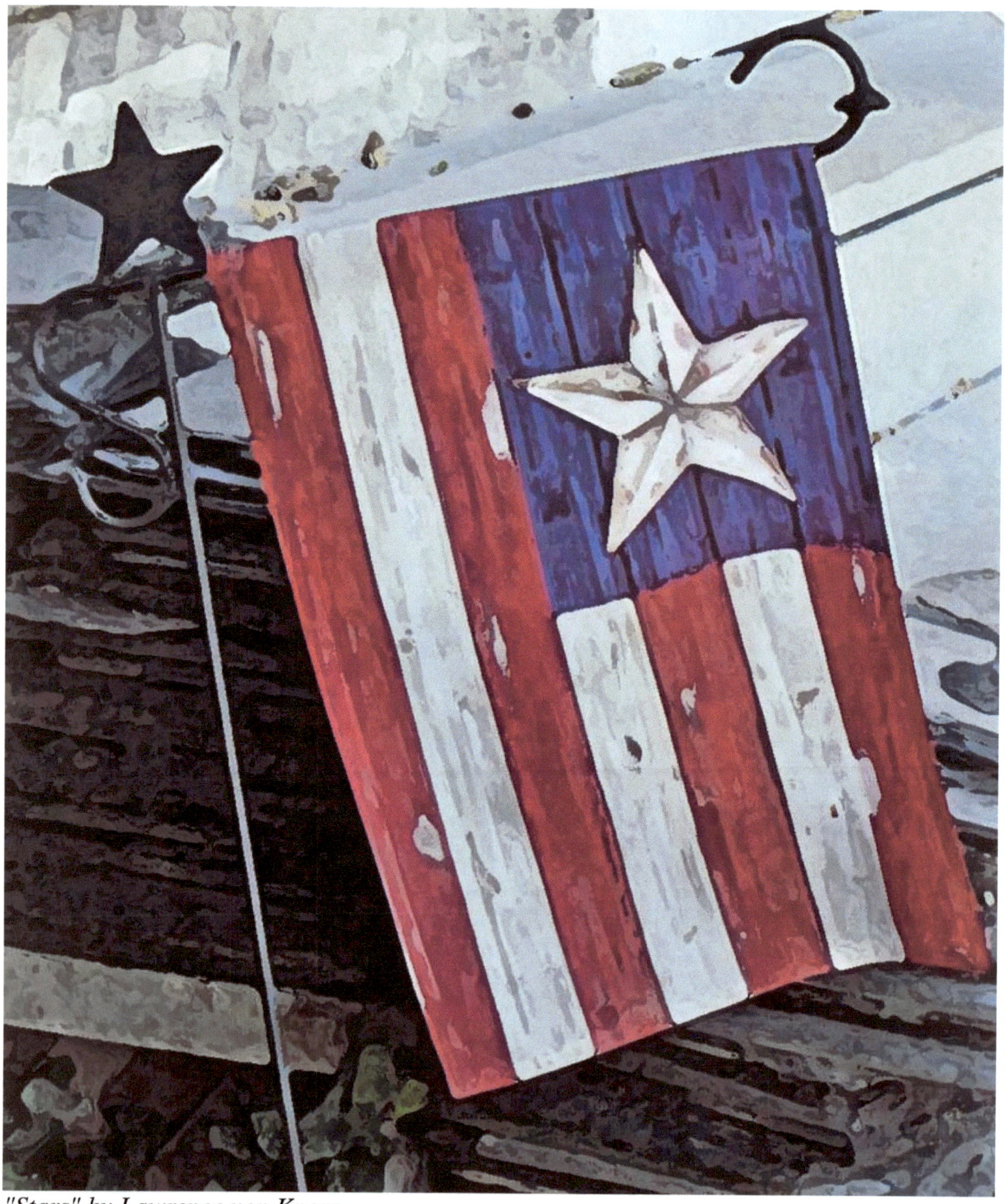

"Stars" by Lawrence von Knorr

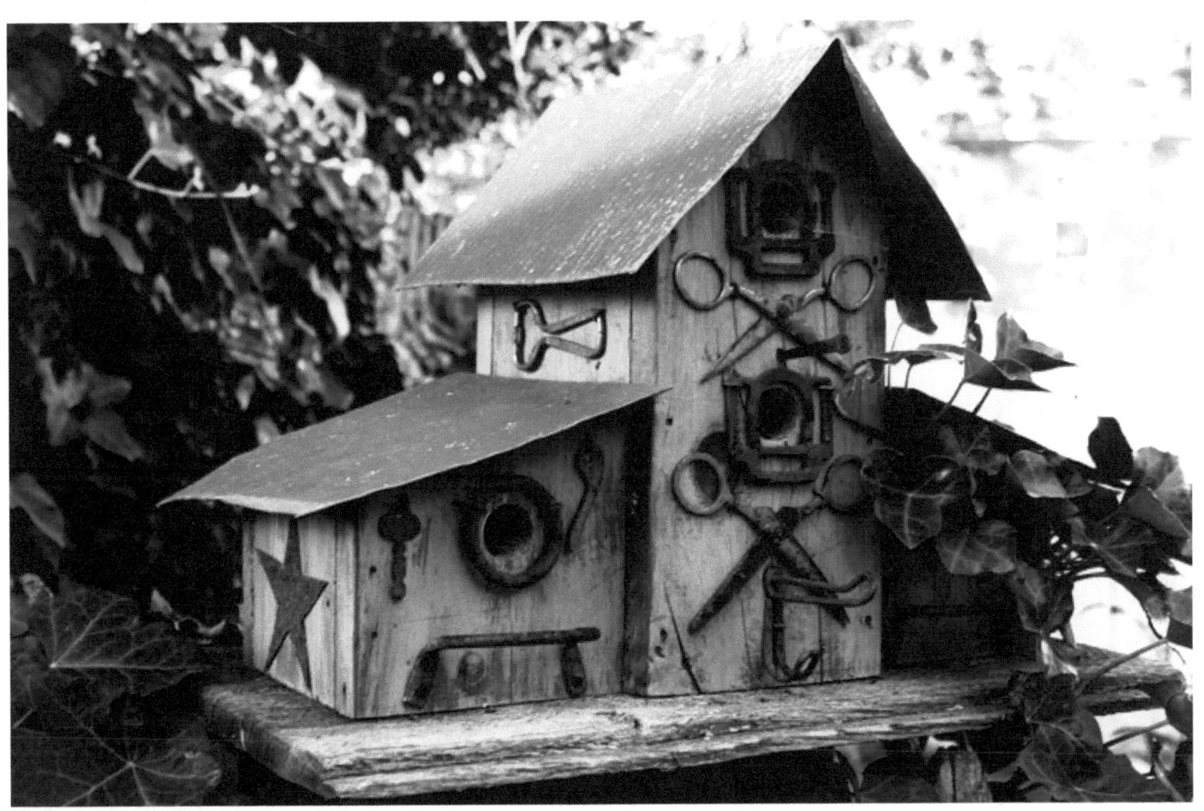

"Bird House" by Tammi Knorr

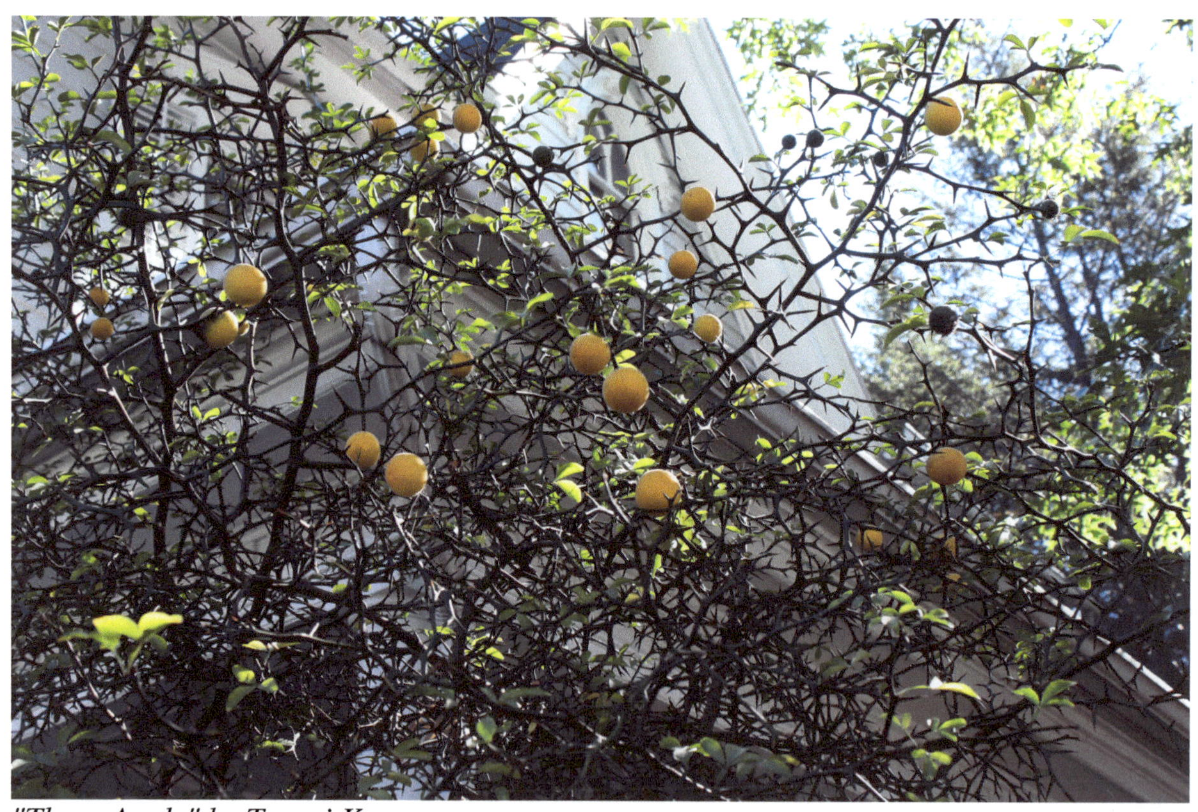

"Thorn Apple" by Tammi Knorr

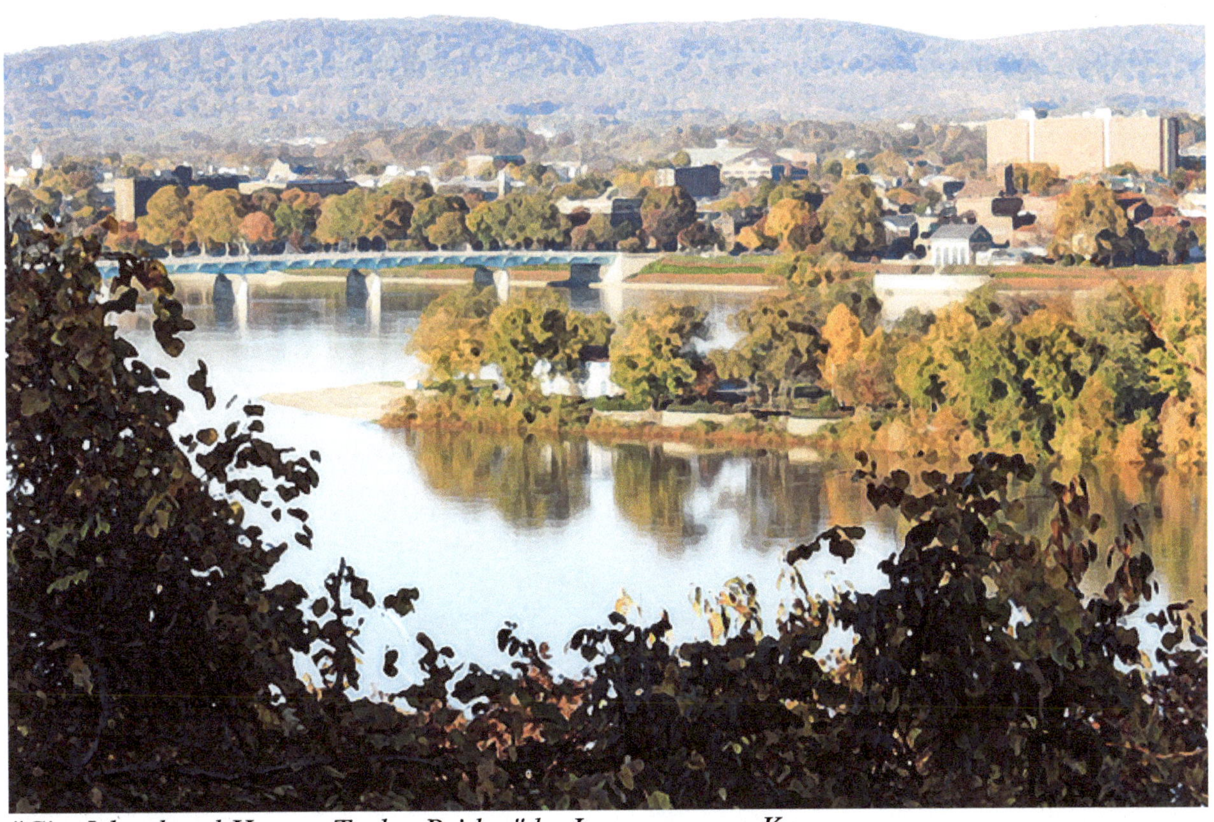

"City Island and Harvey Taylor Bridge" by Lawrence von Knorr

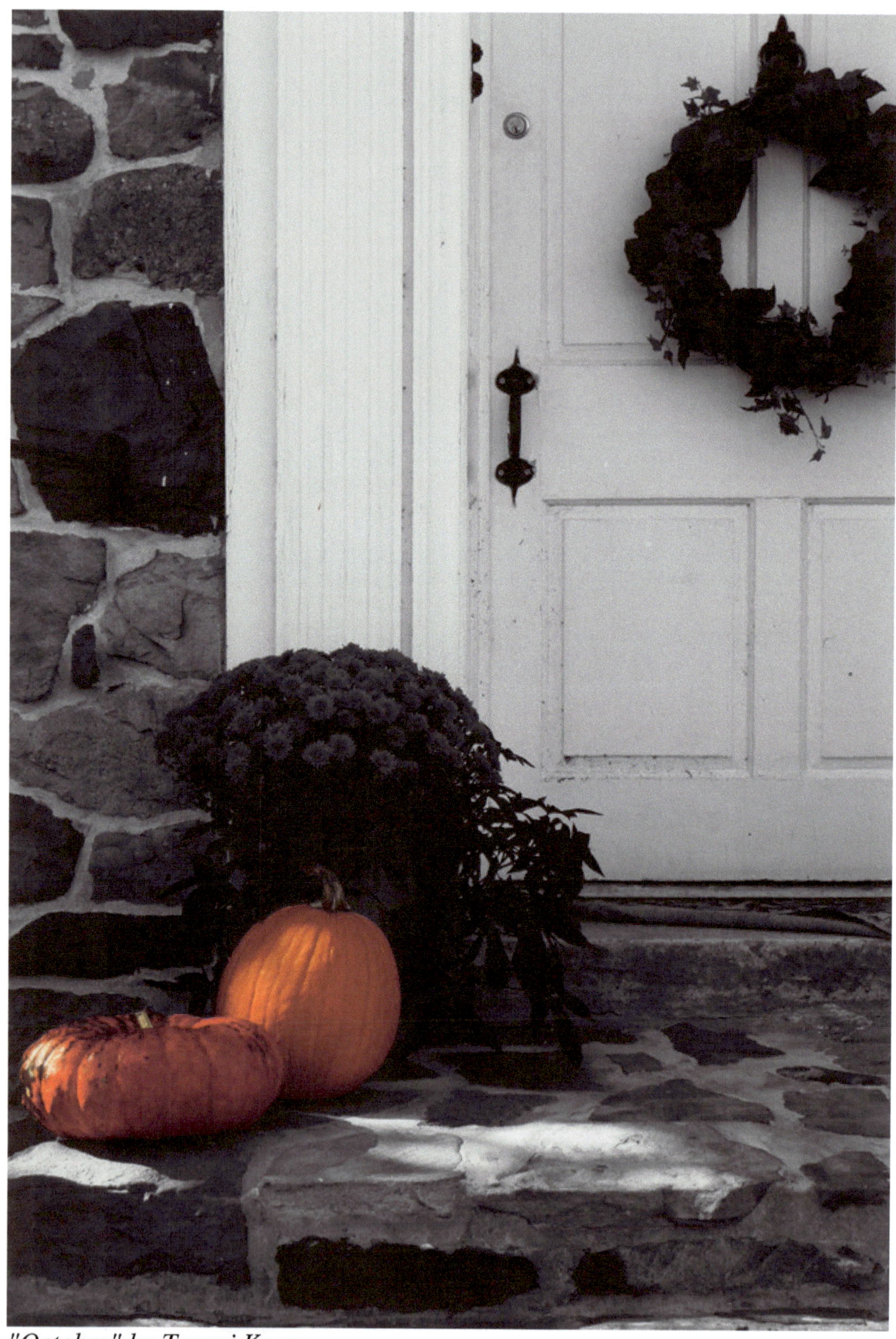

"October" by Tammi Knorr

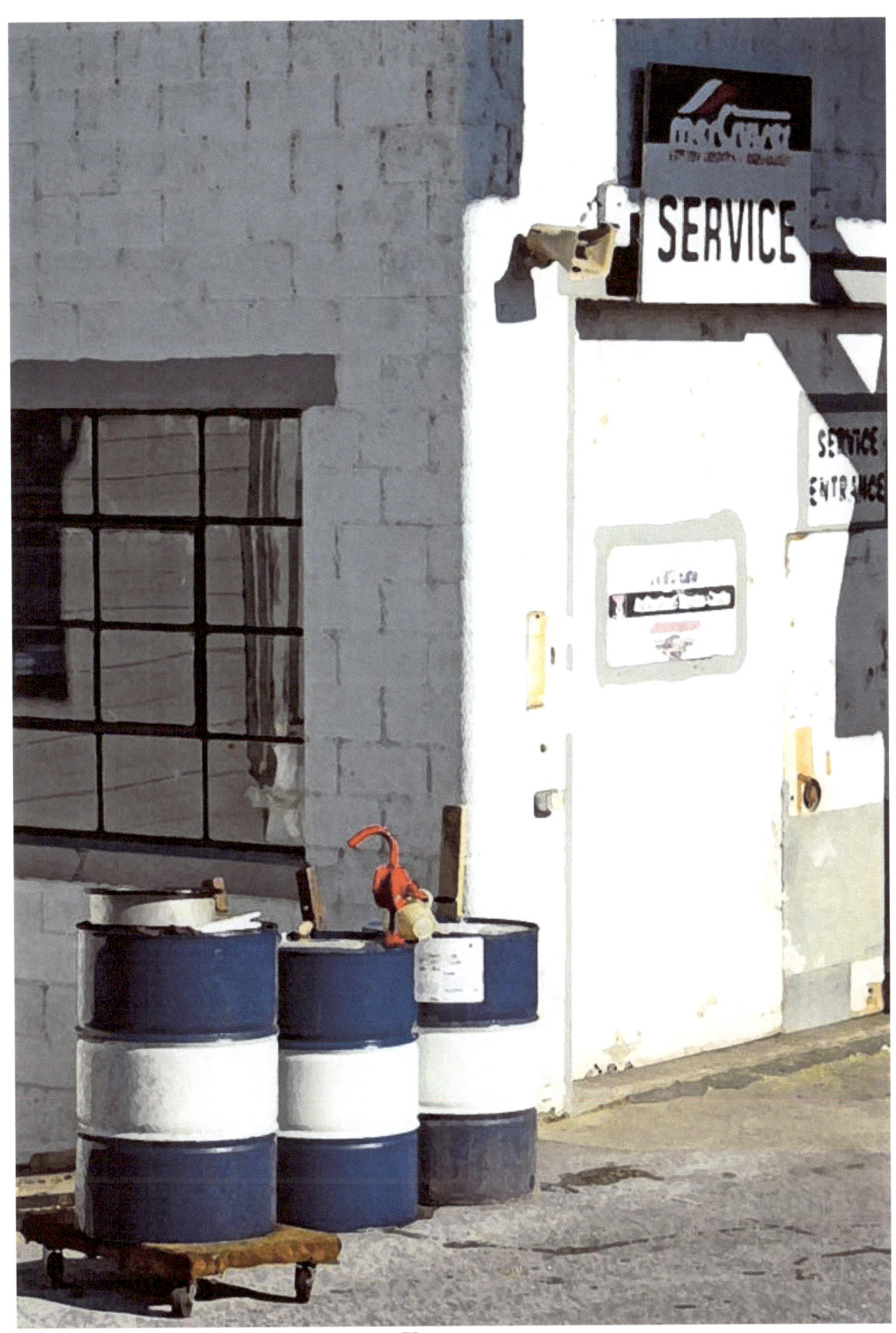

"Service Station" by Lawrence von Knorr

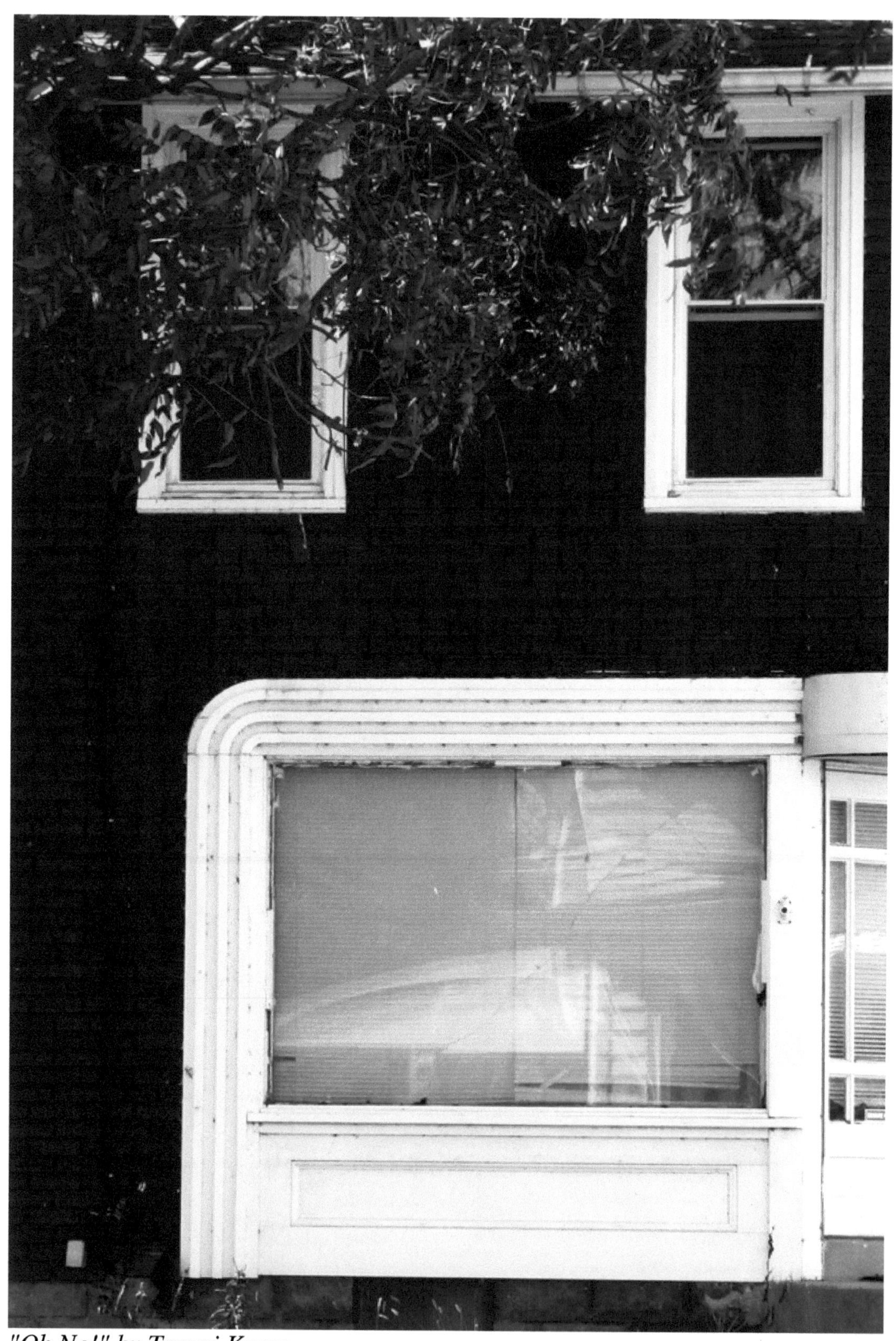

"Oh No!" by Tammi Knorr

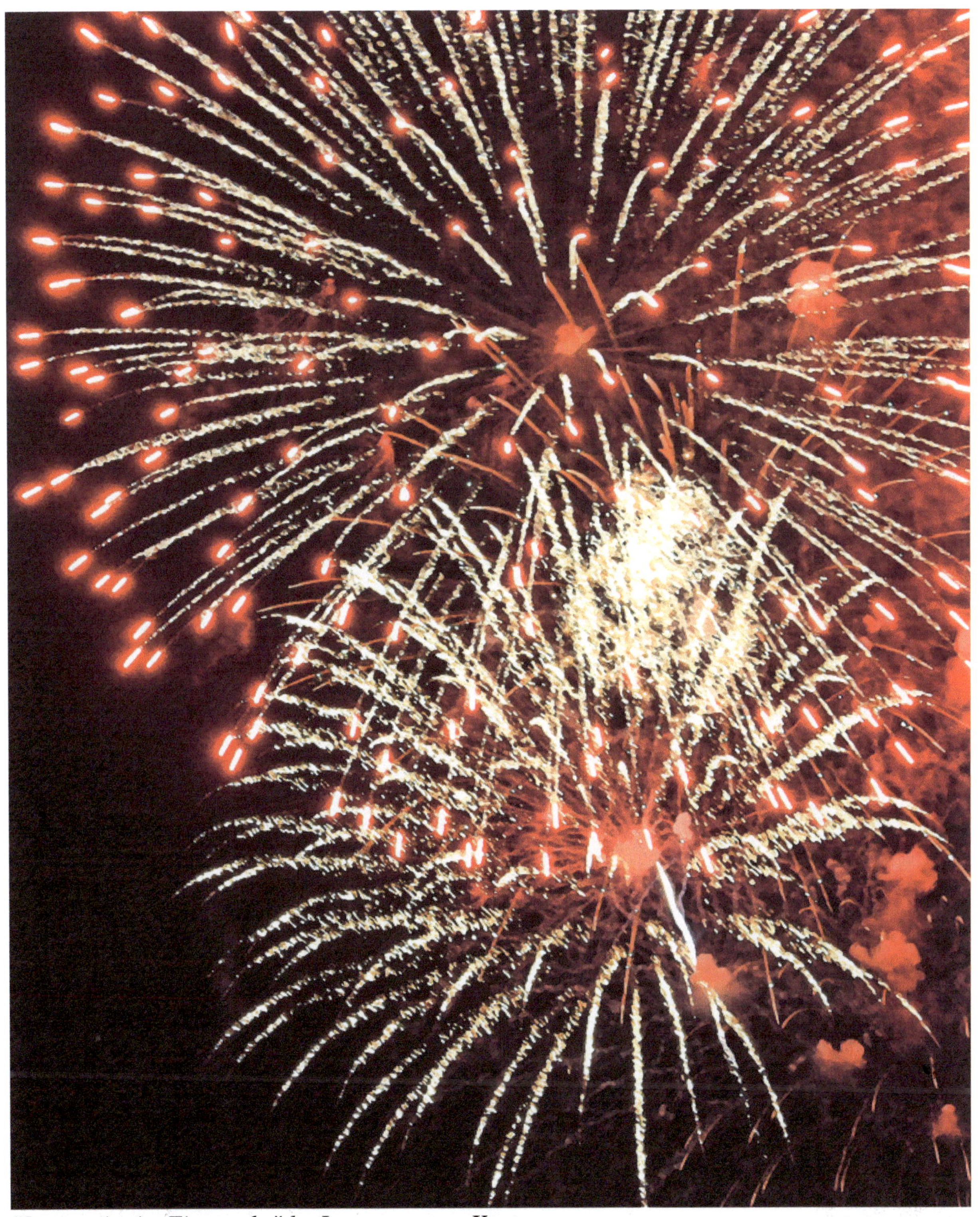

"Impressionist Fireworks" by Lawrence von Knorr

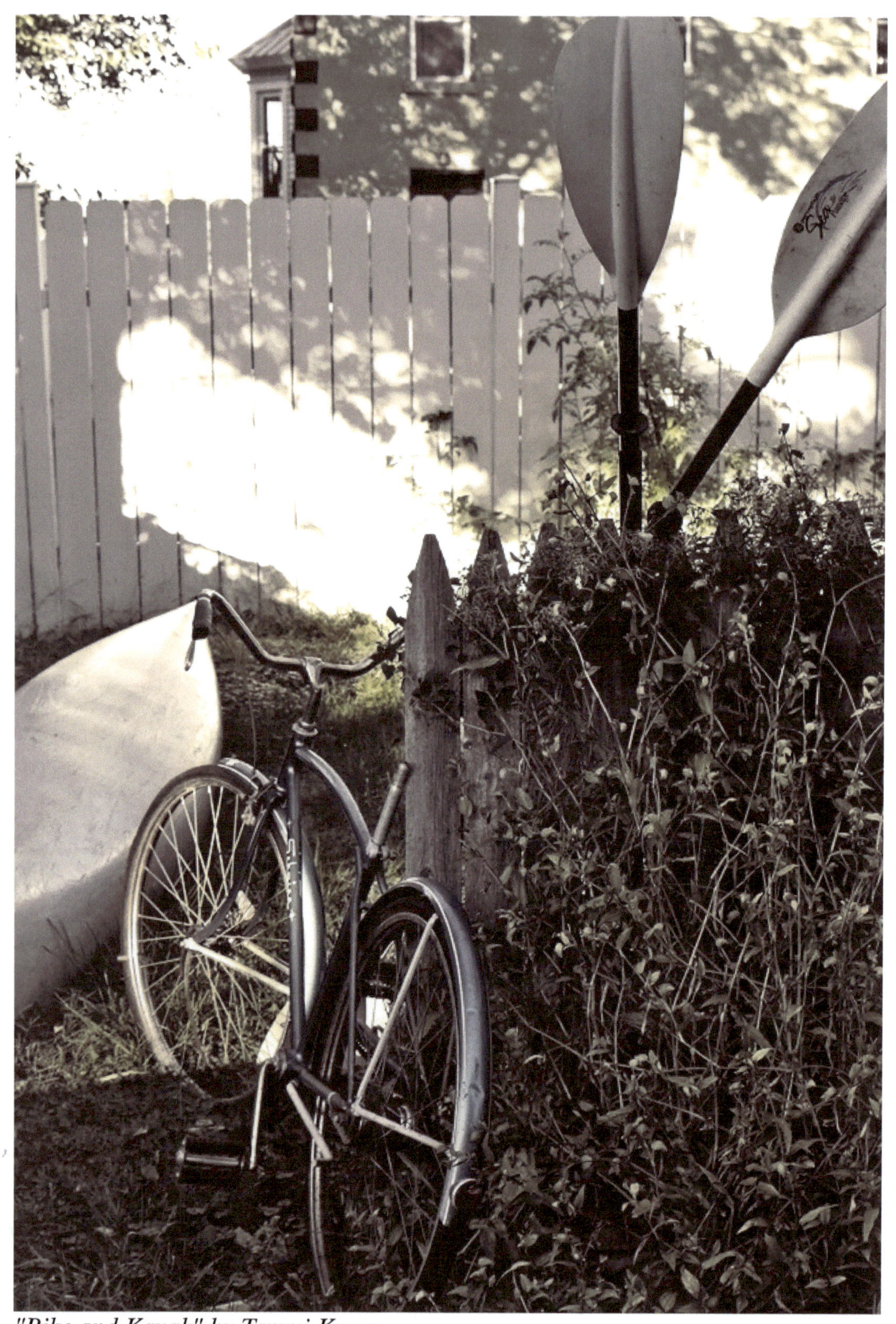

"Bike and Kayak" by Tammi Knorr

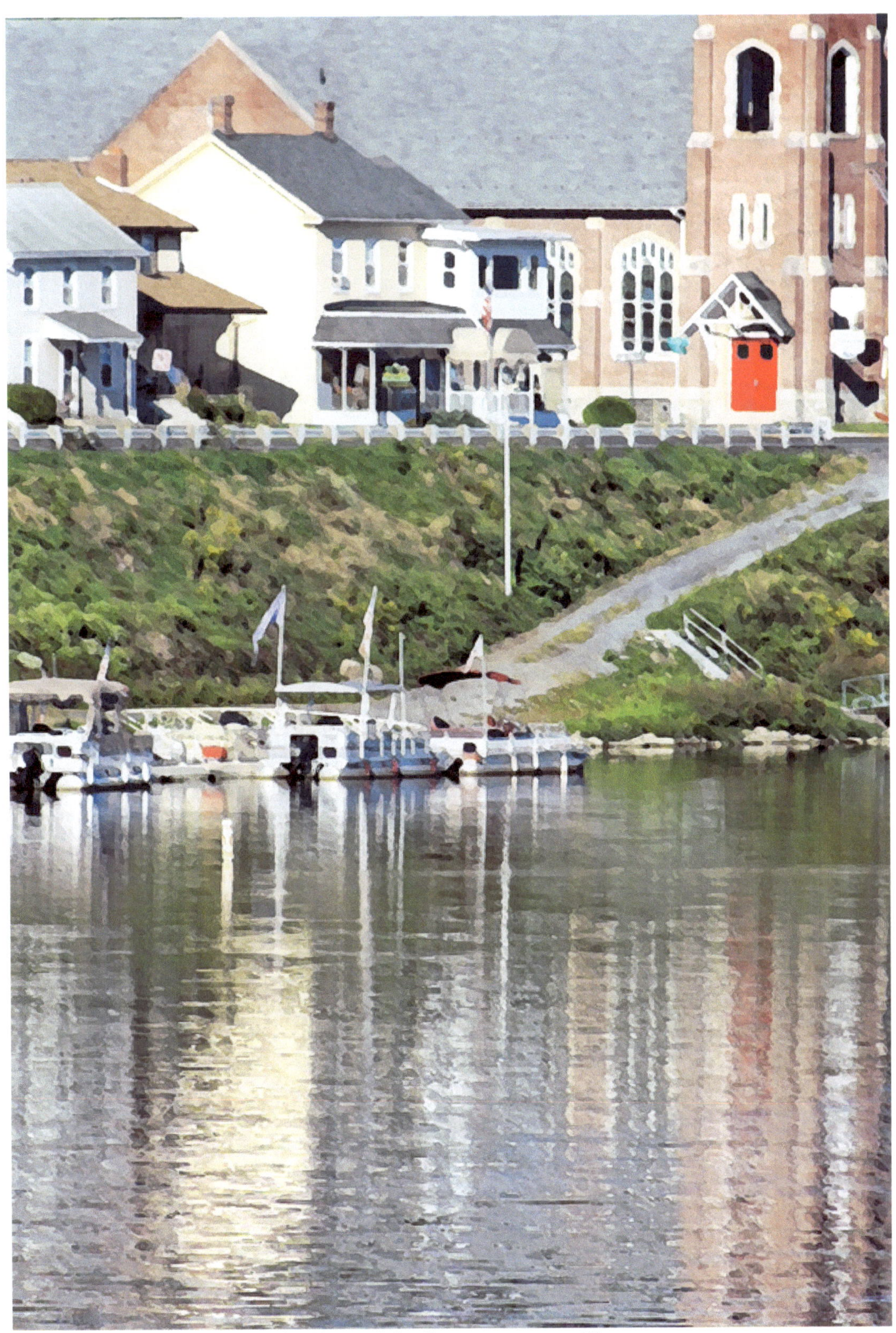

"West Shore Gallery by the Water" by Lawrence von Knorr

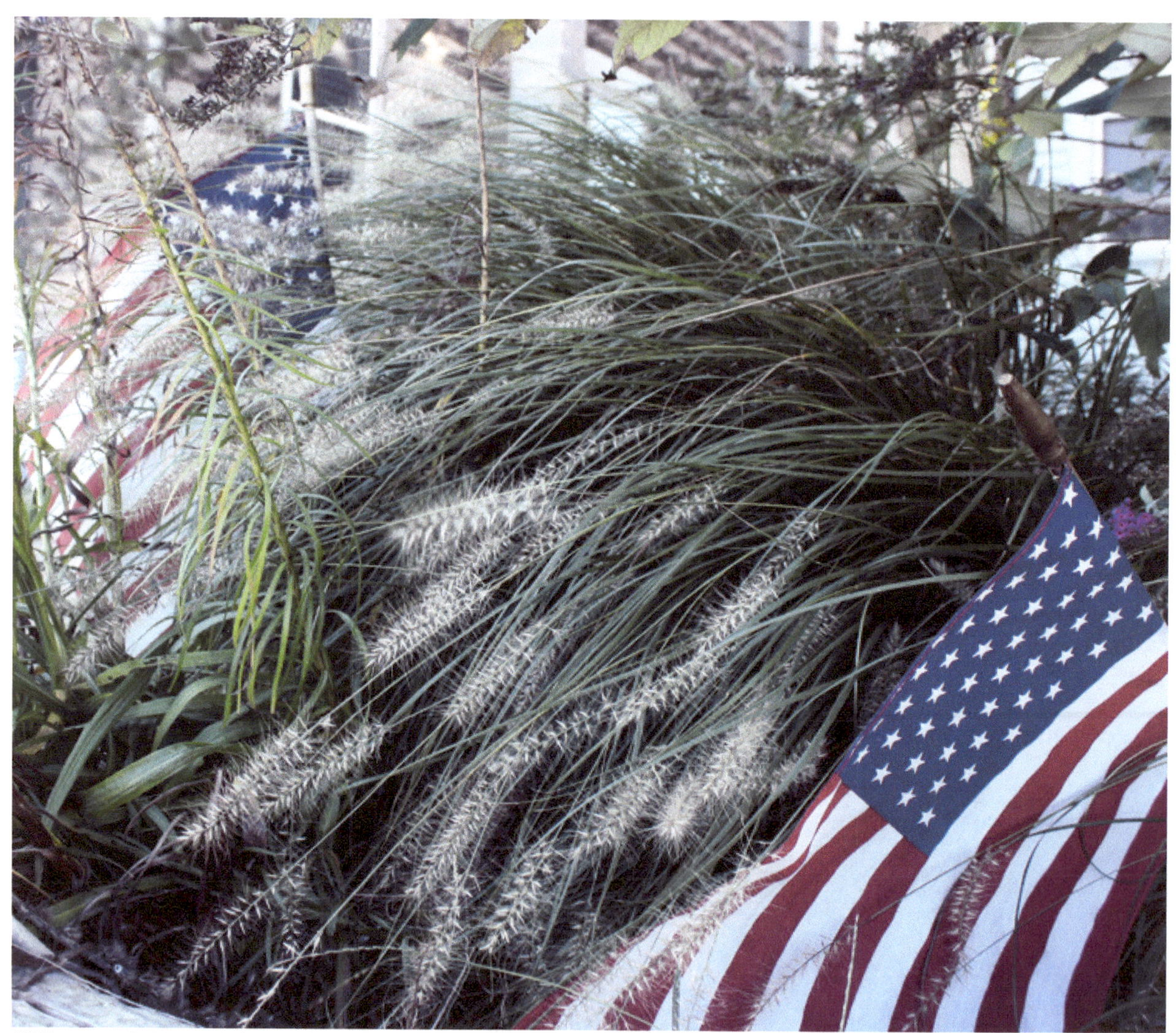

"Waves of Grain" by Tammi Knorr

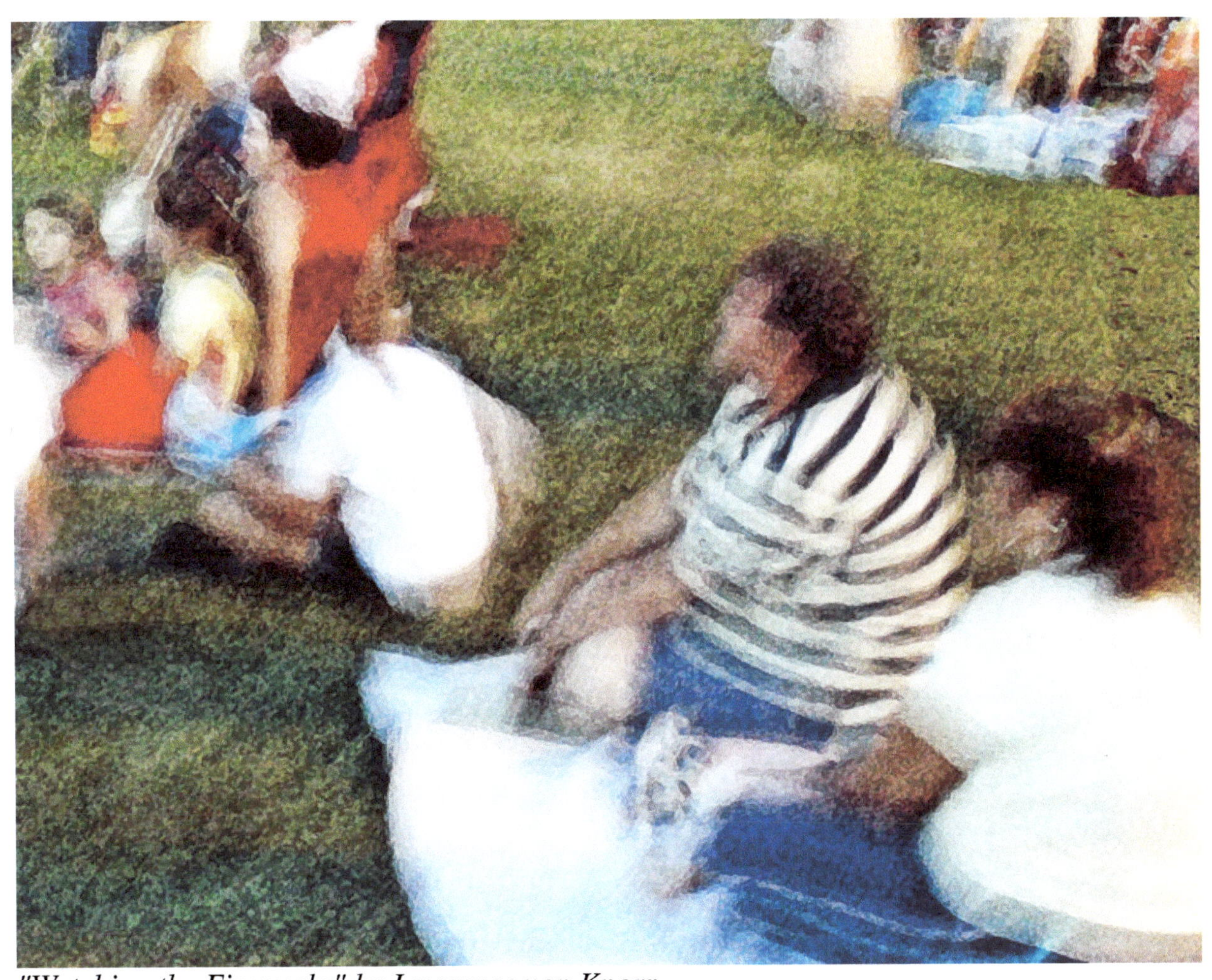

"Watching the Fireworks" by Lawrence von Knorr

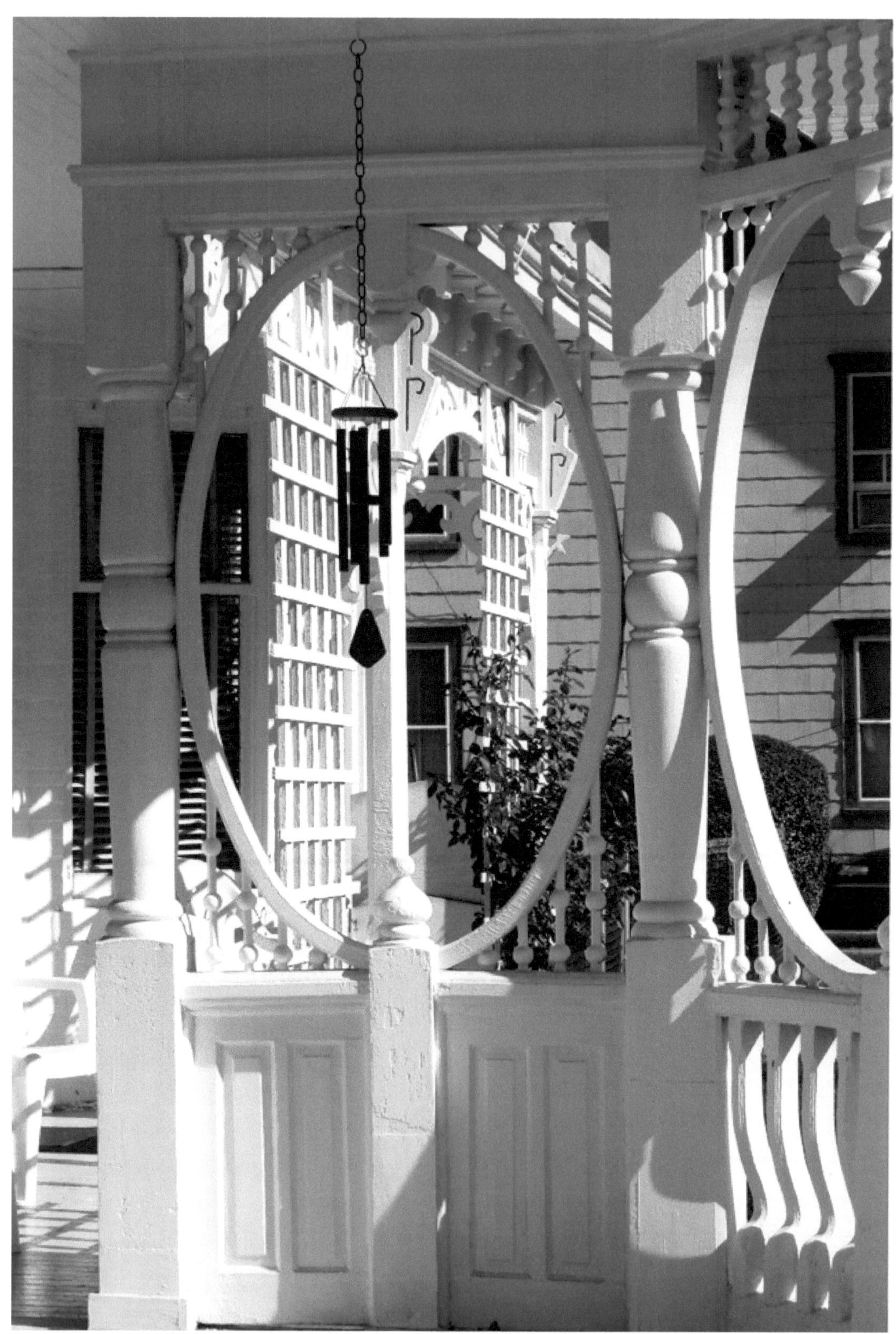

"Gingerbread Porch" by Tammi Knorr

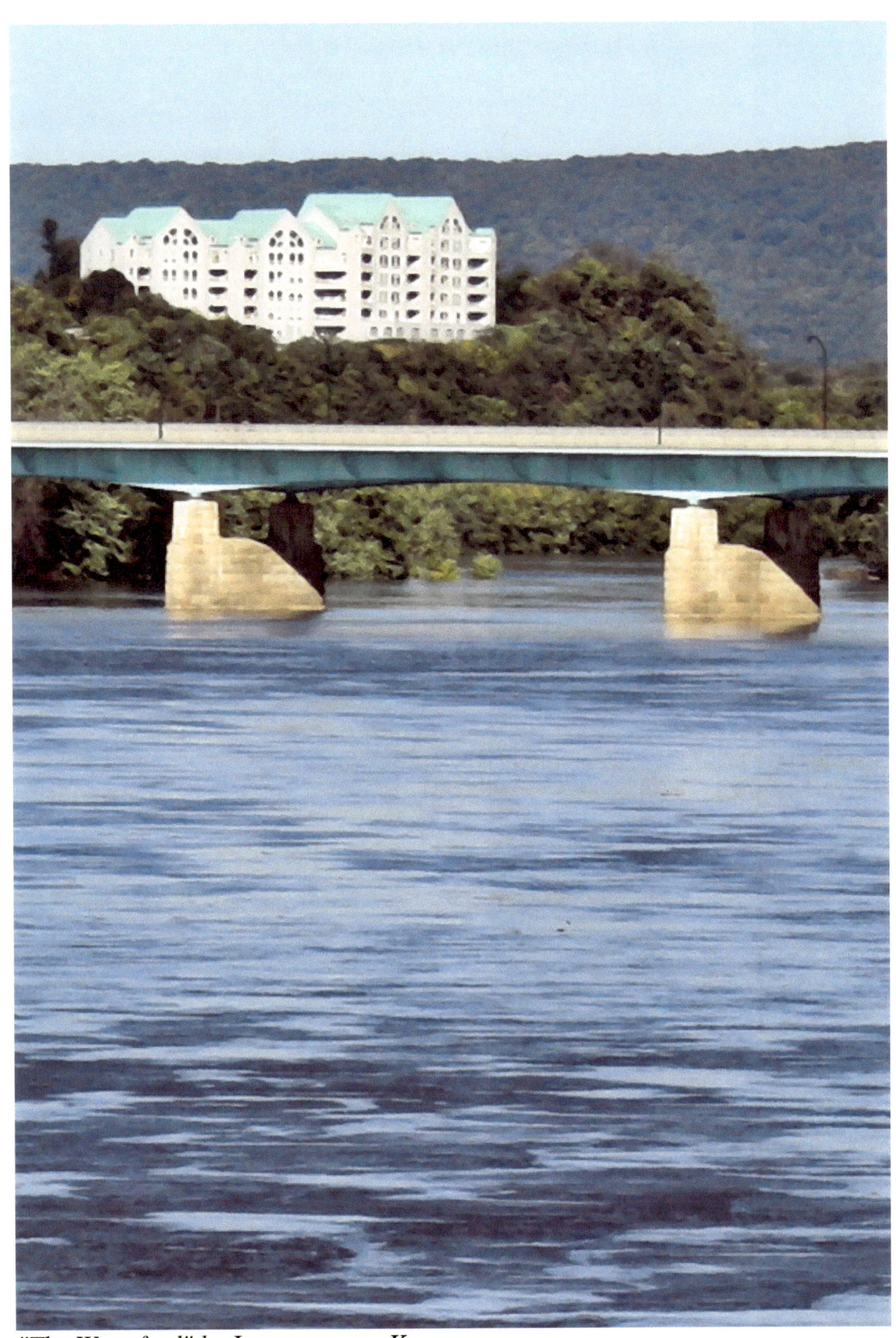

"The Waterford" by Lawrence von Knorr

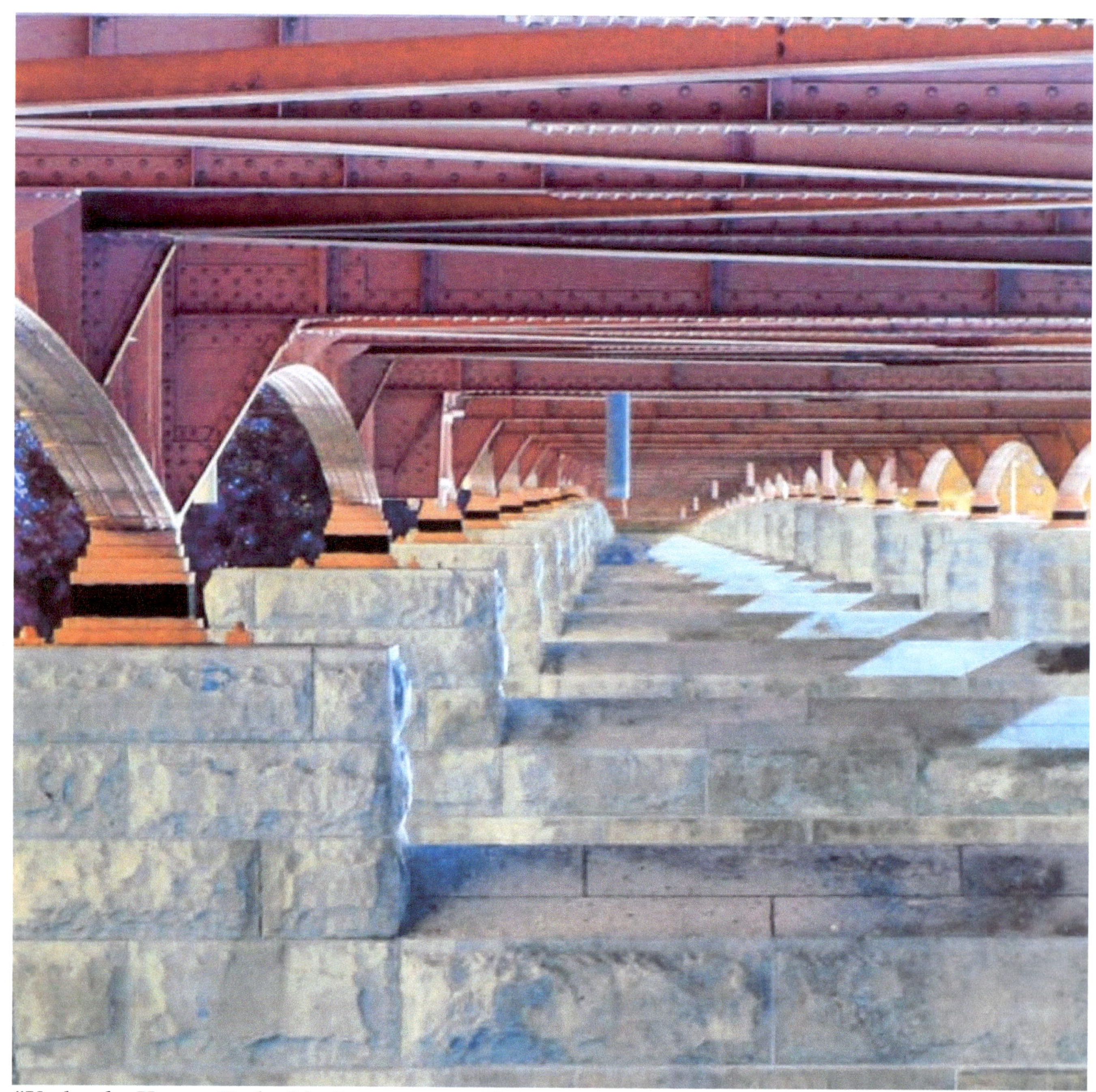

"Under the Harvey Taylor" by Lawrence von Knorr

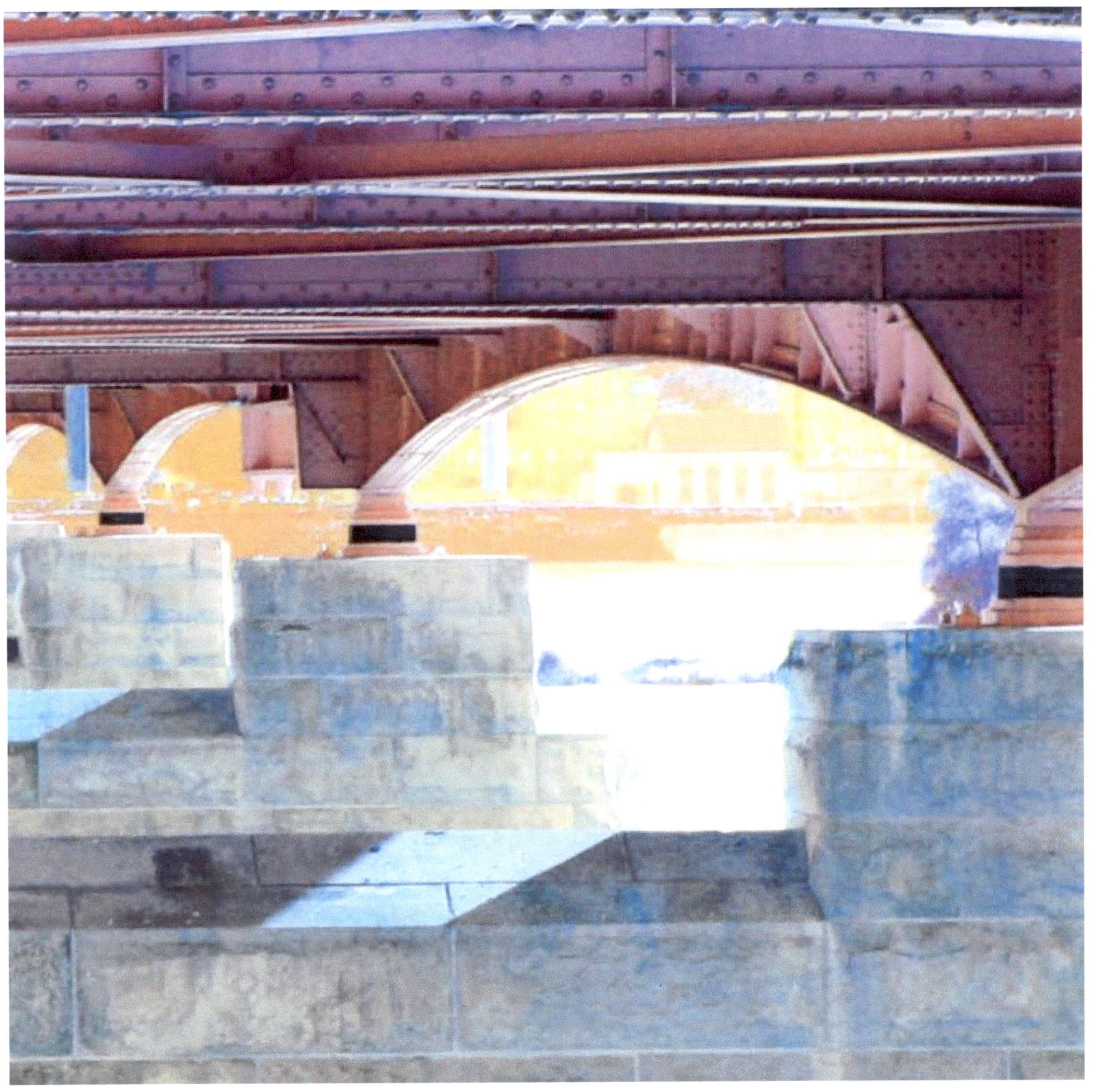

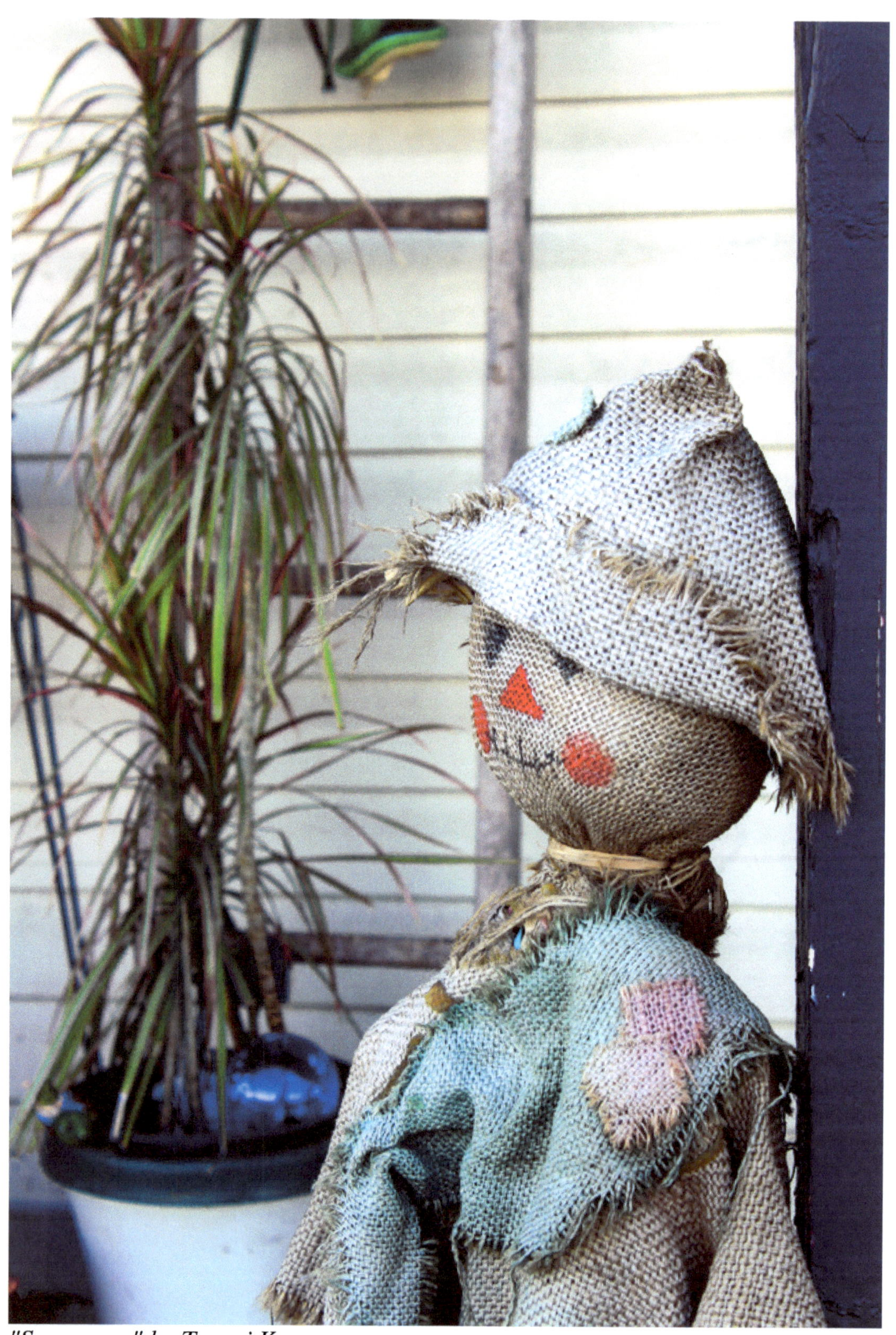

"Scarecrow" by Tammi Knorr

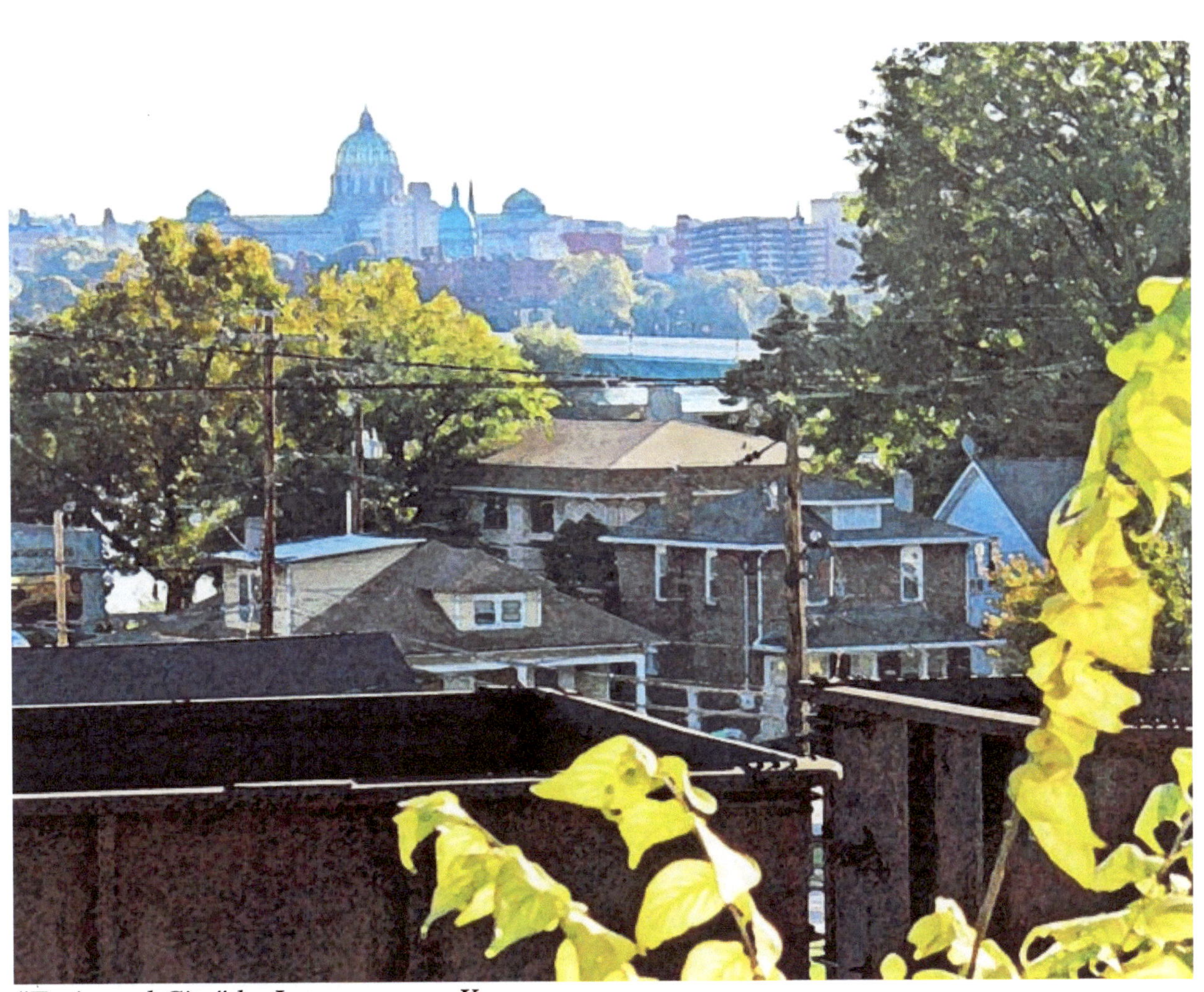

"Train and City" by Lawrence von Knorr

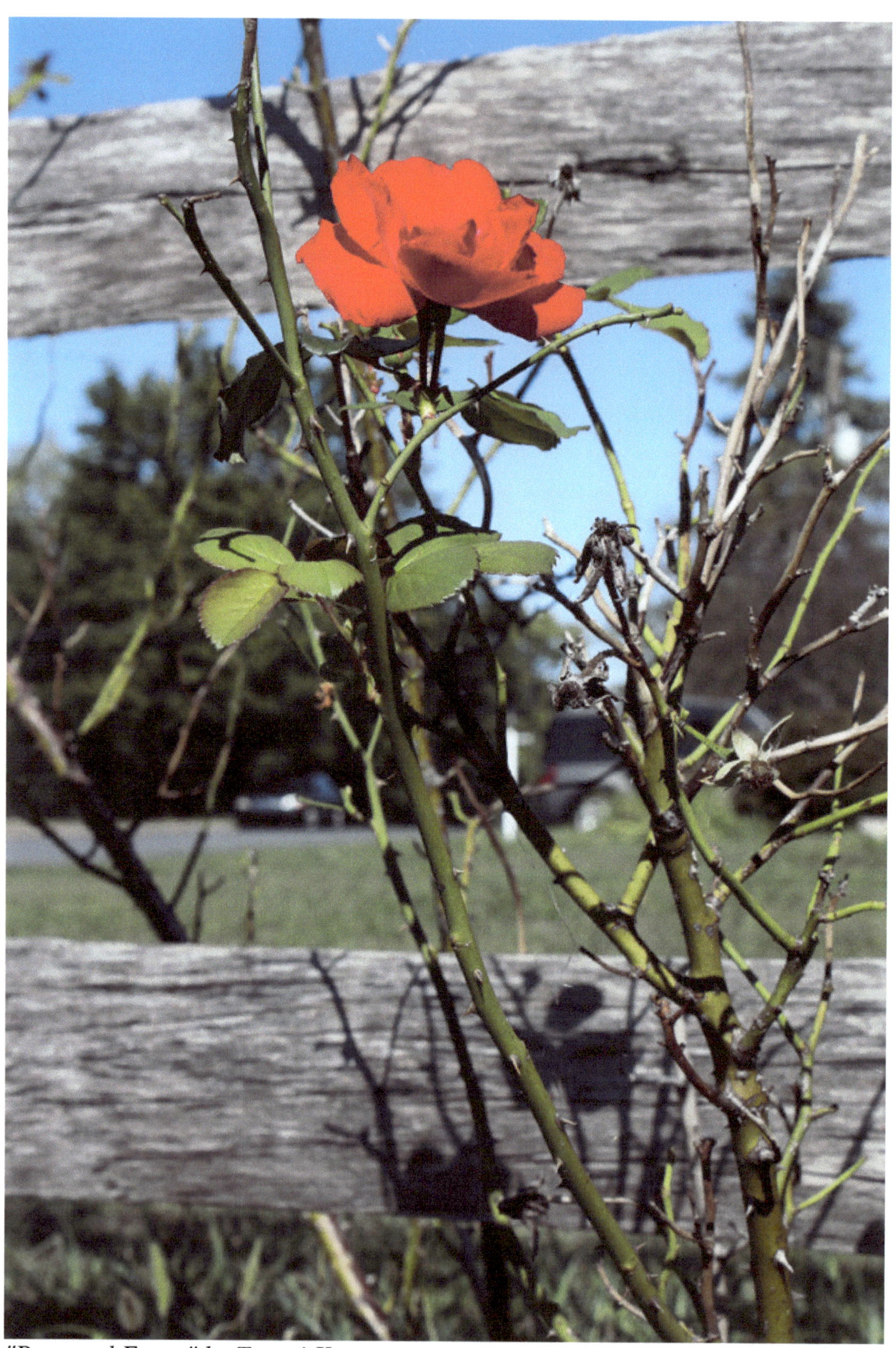

"Rose and Fence" by Tammi Knorr

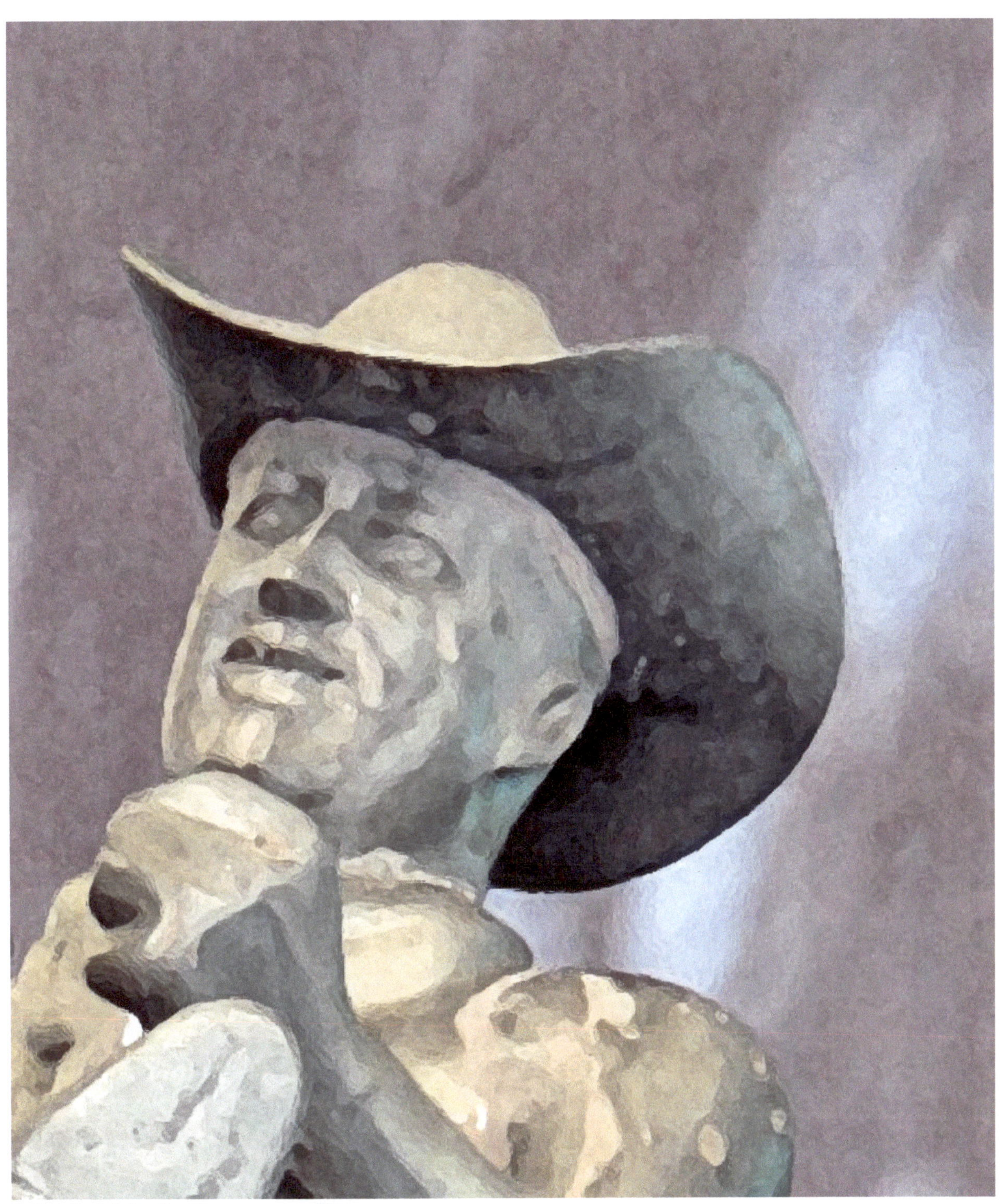

"Cowboy" by Lawrence von Knorr

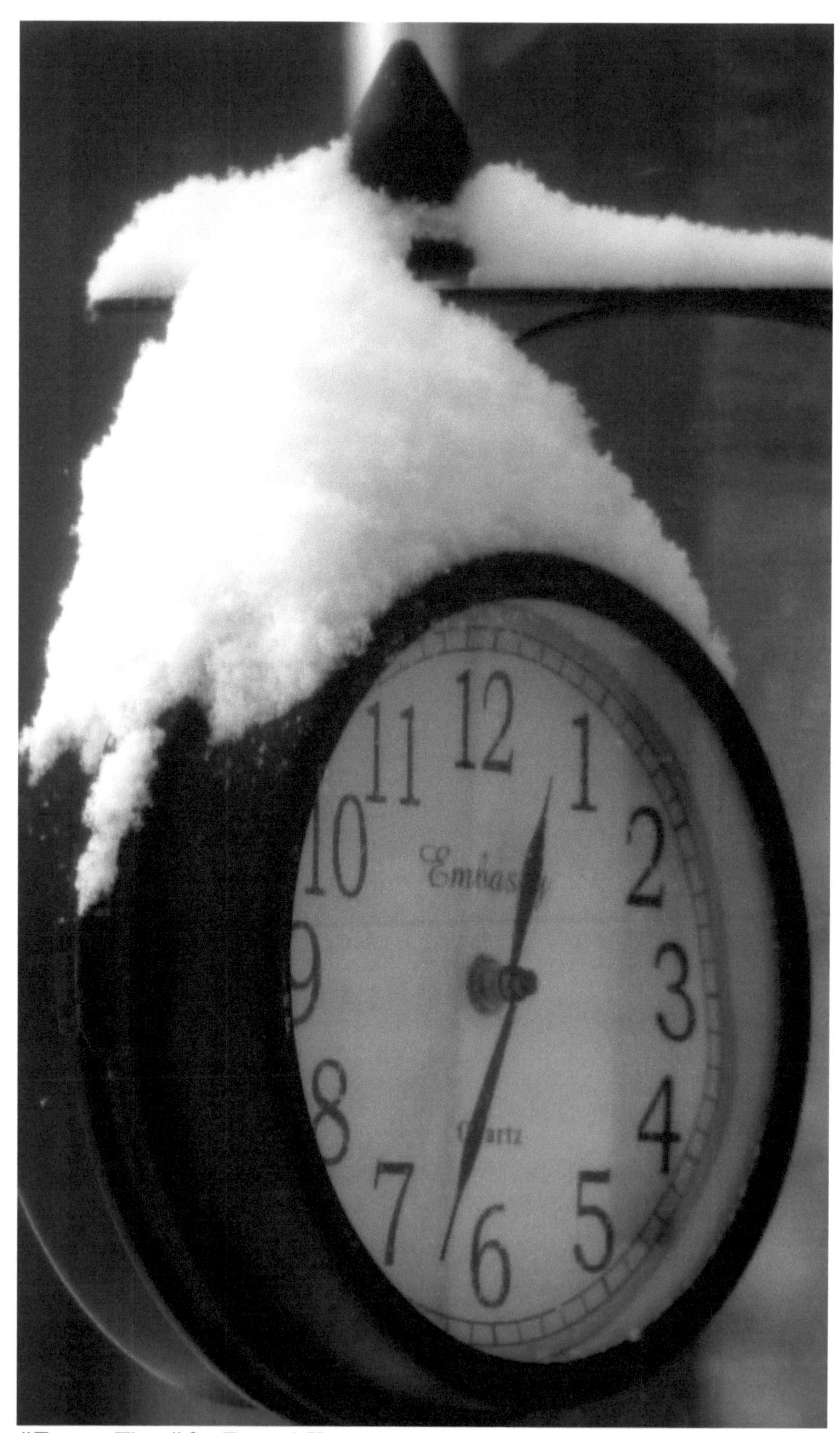

"Freeze Time" by Tammi Knorr

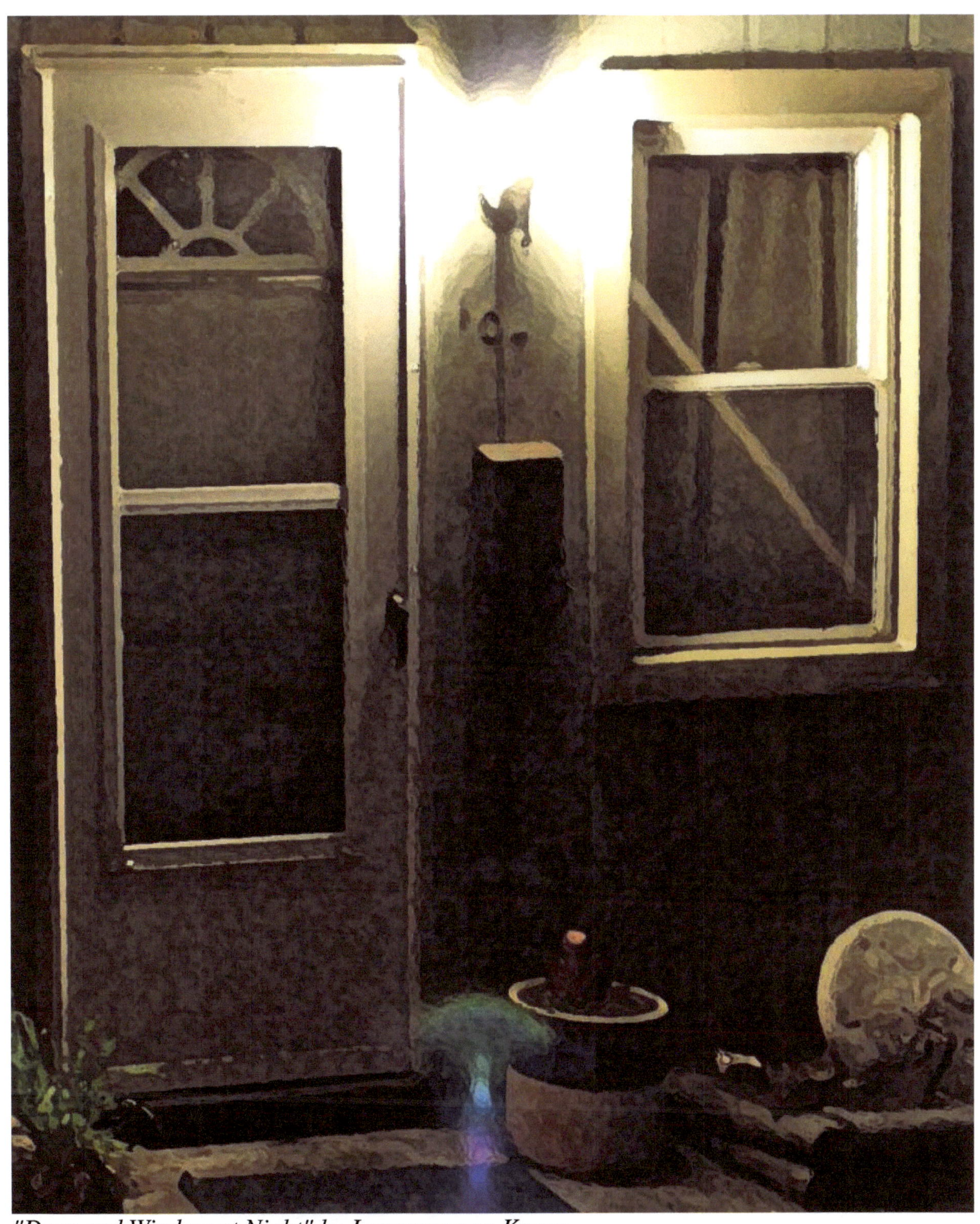

"Door and Window at Night" by Lawrence von Knorr

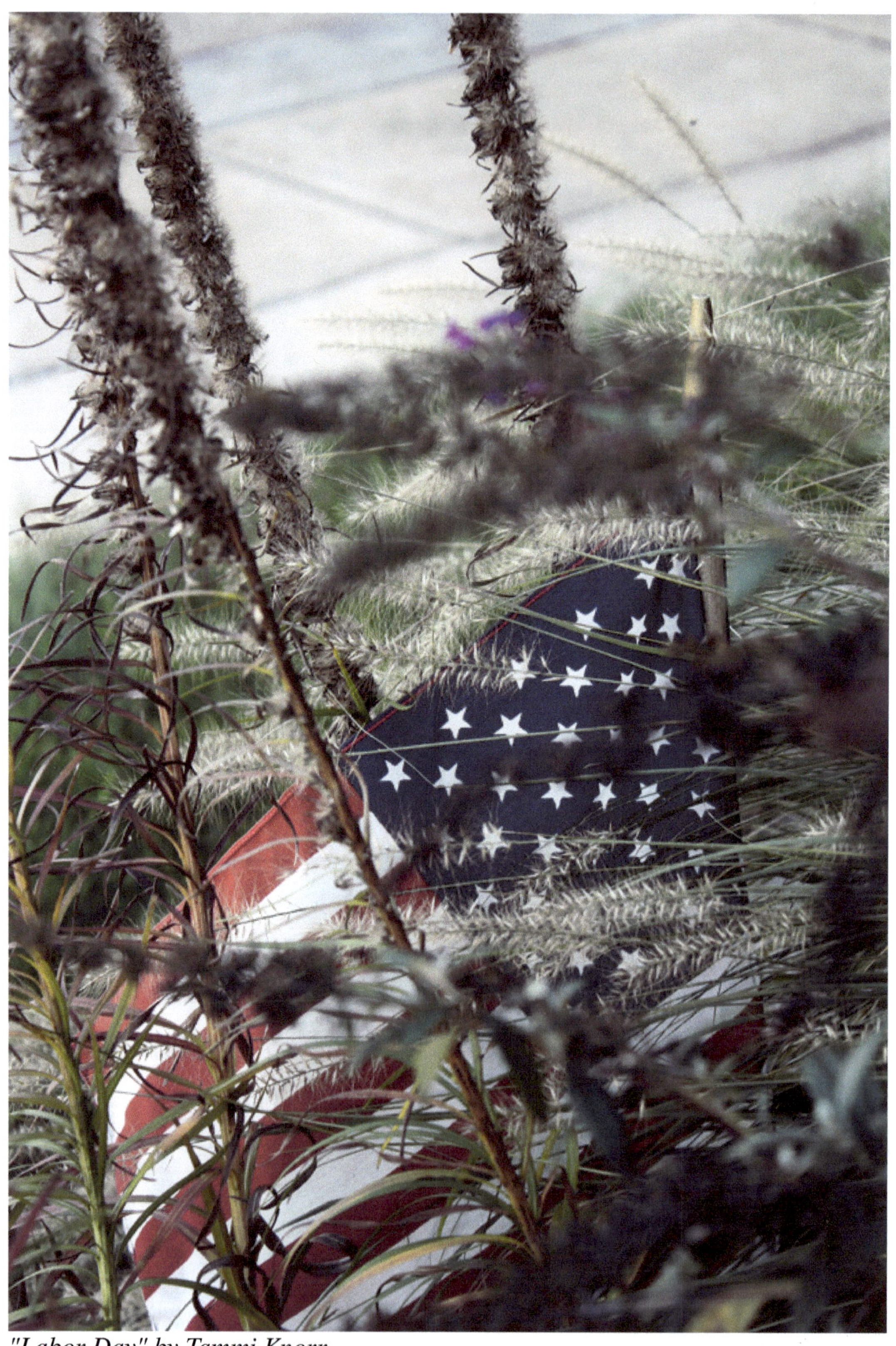

"Labor Day" by Tammi Knorr

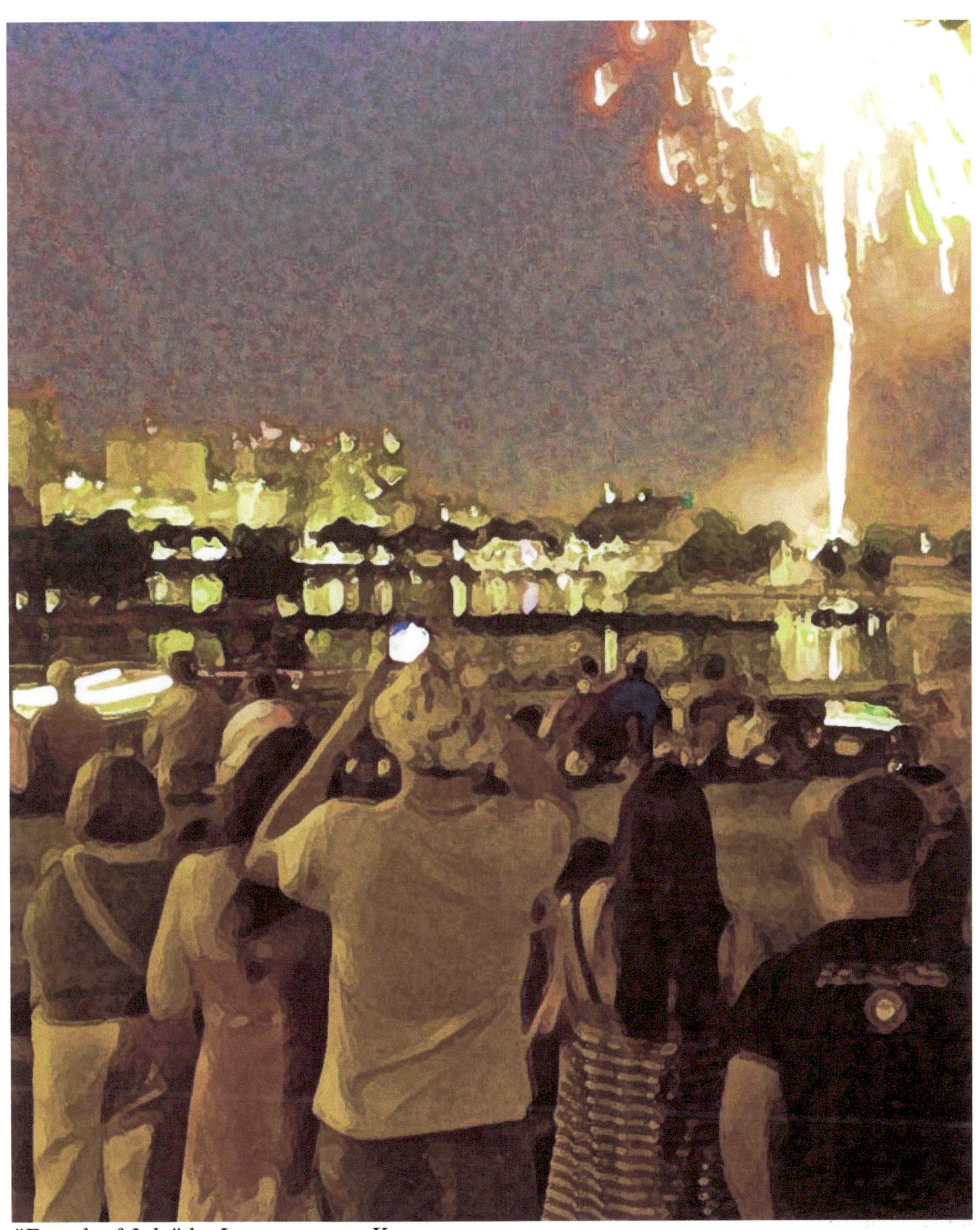

"Fourth of July" by Lawrence von Knorr

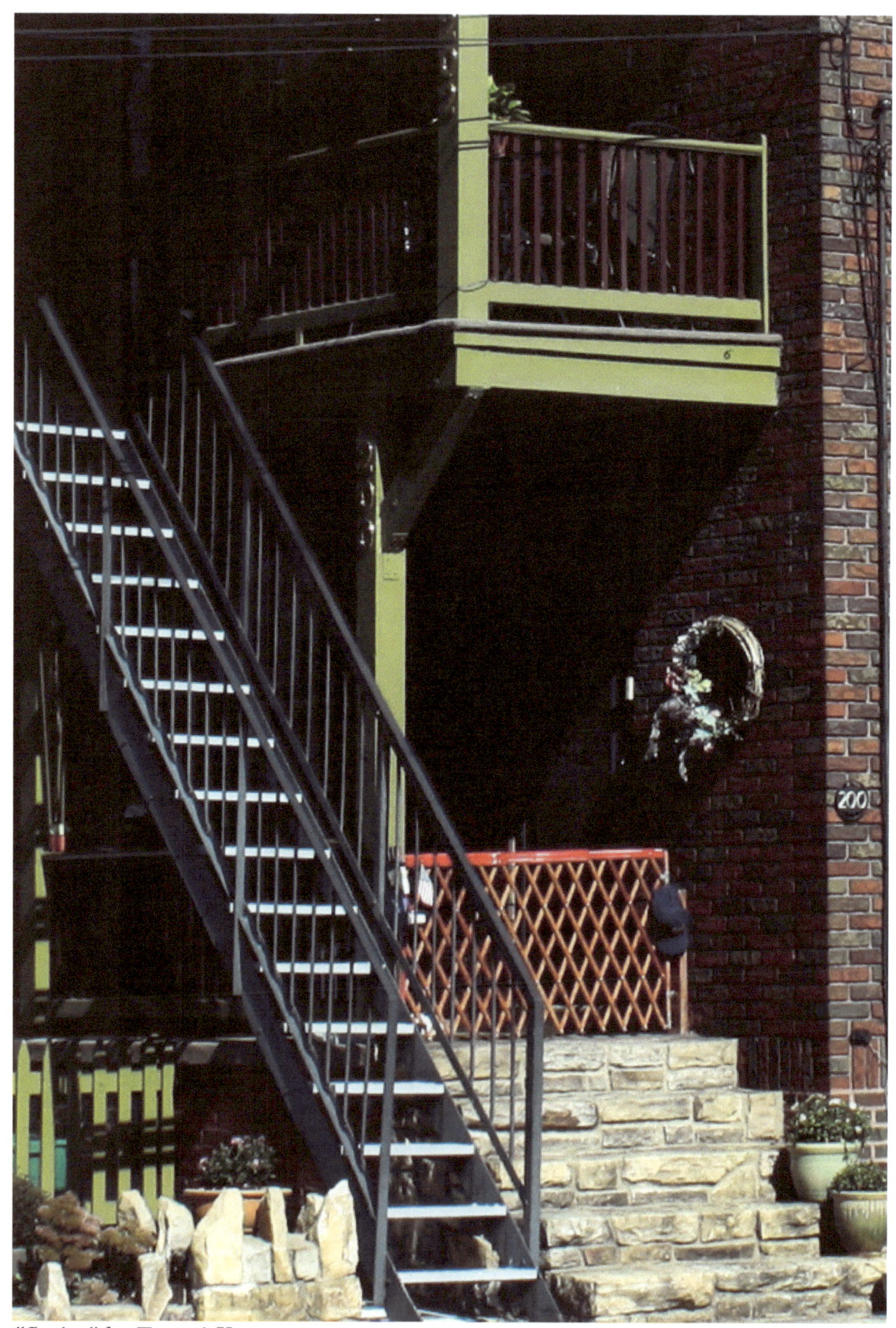

"Stairs" by Tammi Knorr

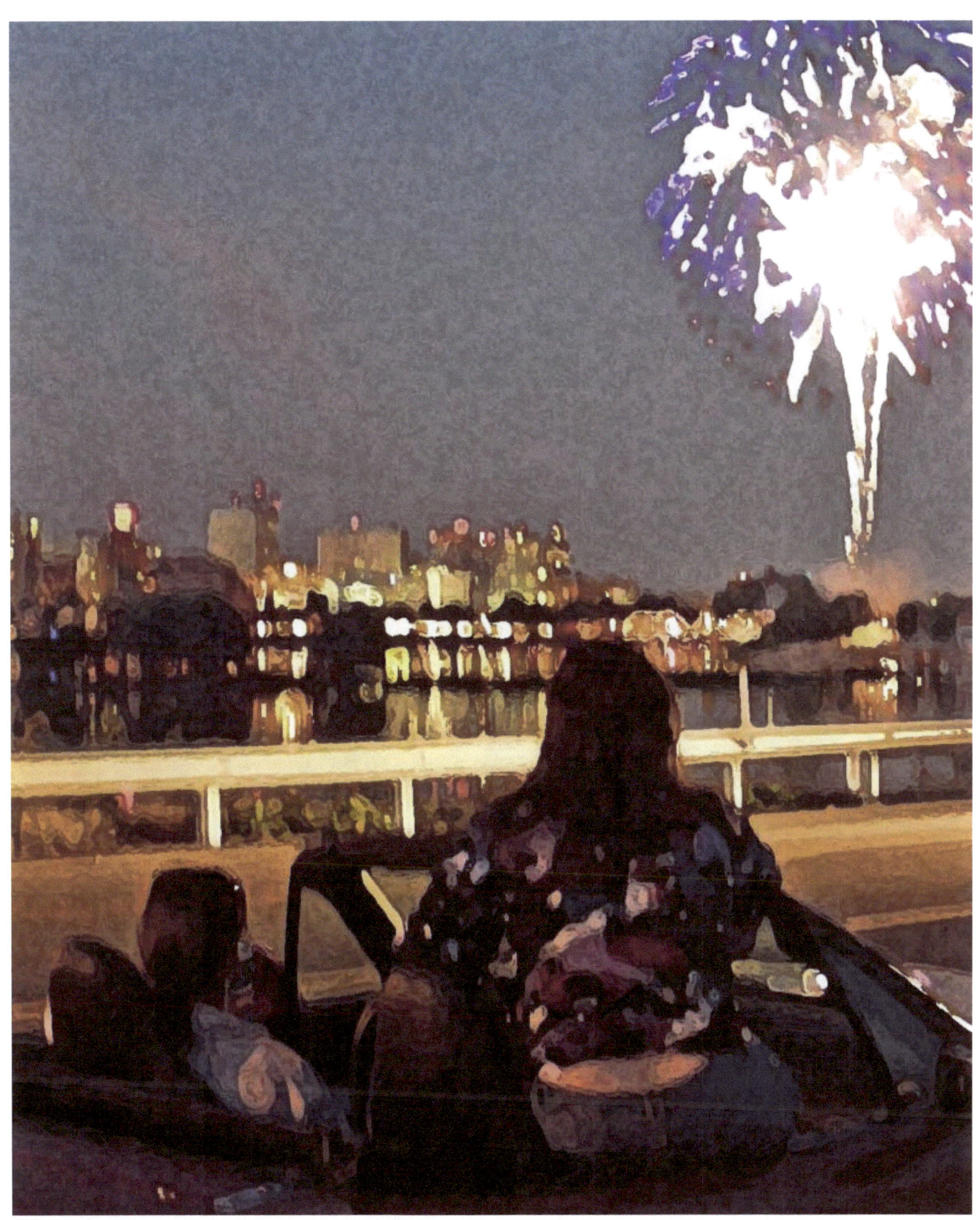

"Fourth of July 2" by Lawrence von Knorr

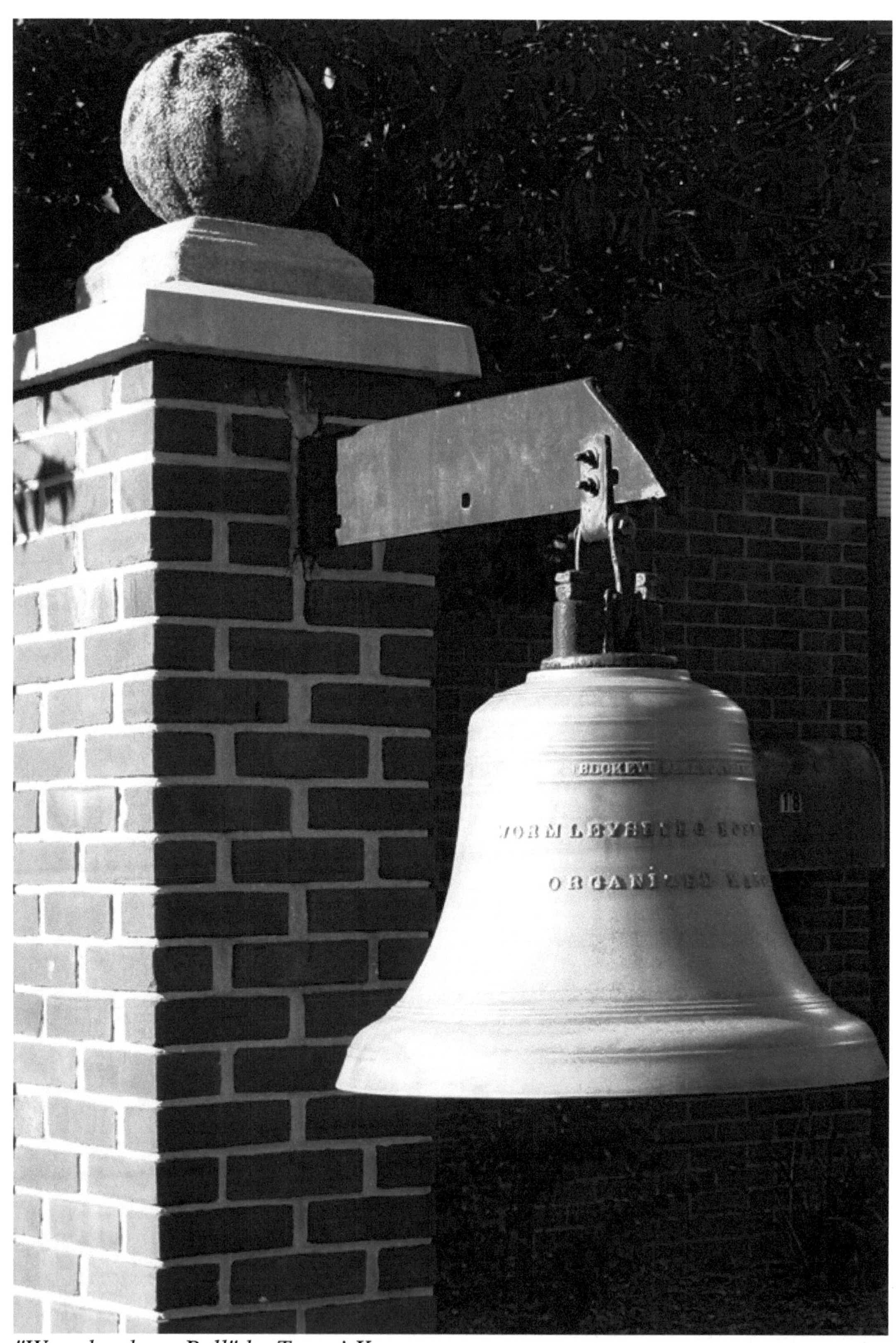

"Wormleysburg Bell" by Tammi Knorr

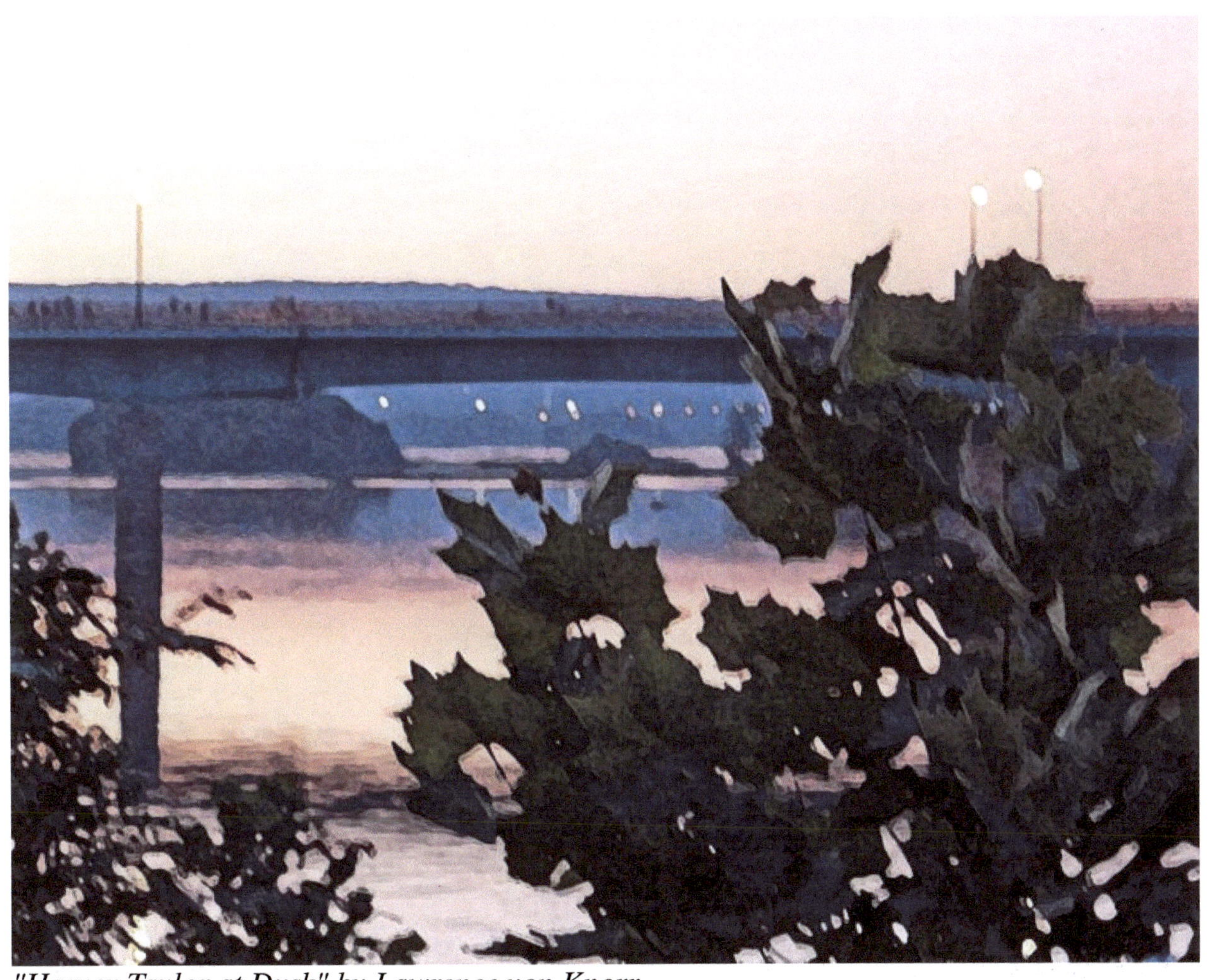
"Harvey Taylor at Dusk" by Lawrence von Knorr

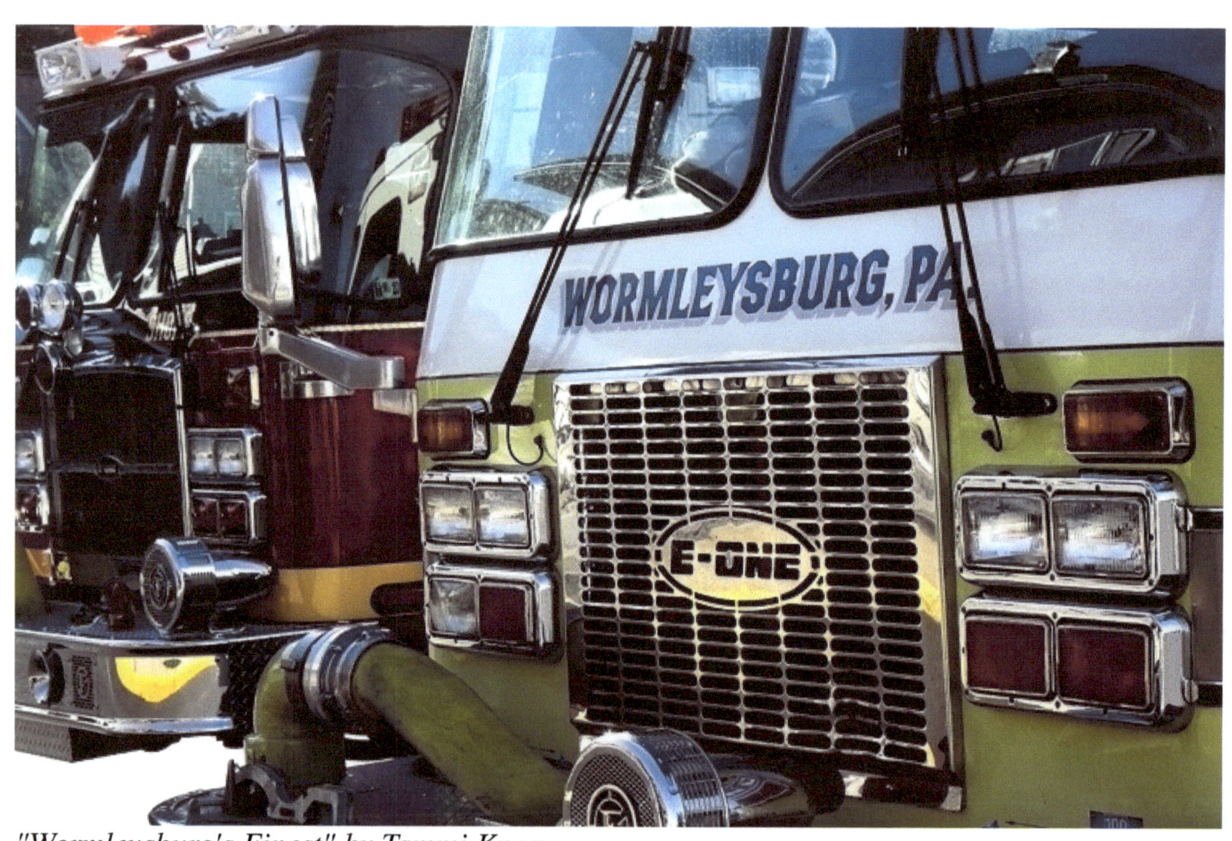

"Wormleysburg's Finest" by Tammi Knorr

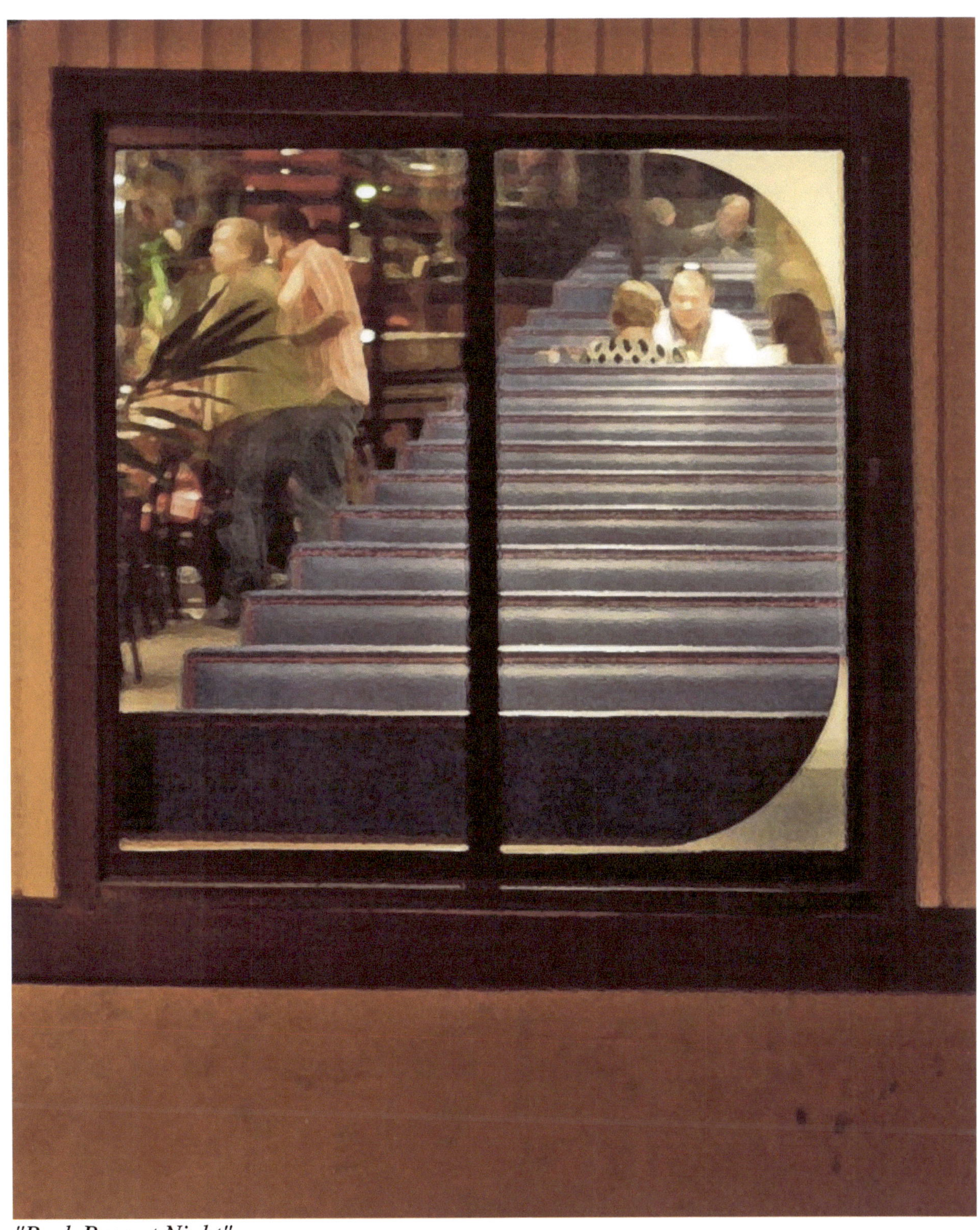

"Rock Bass at Night"

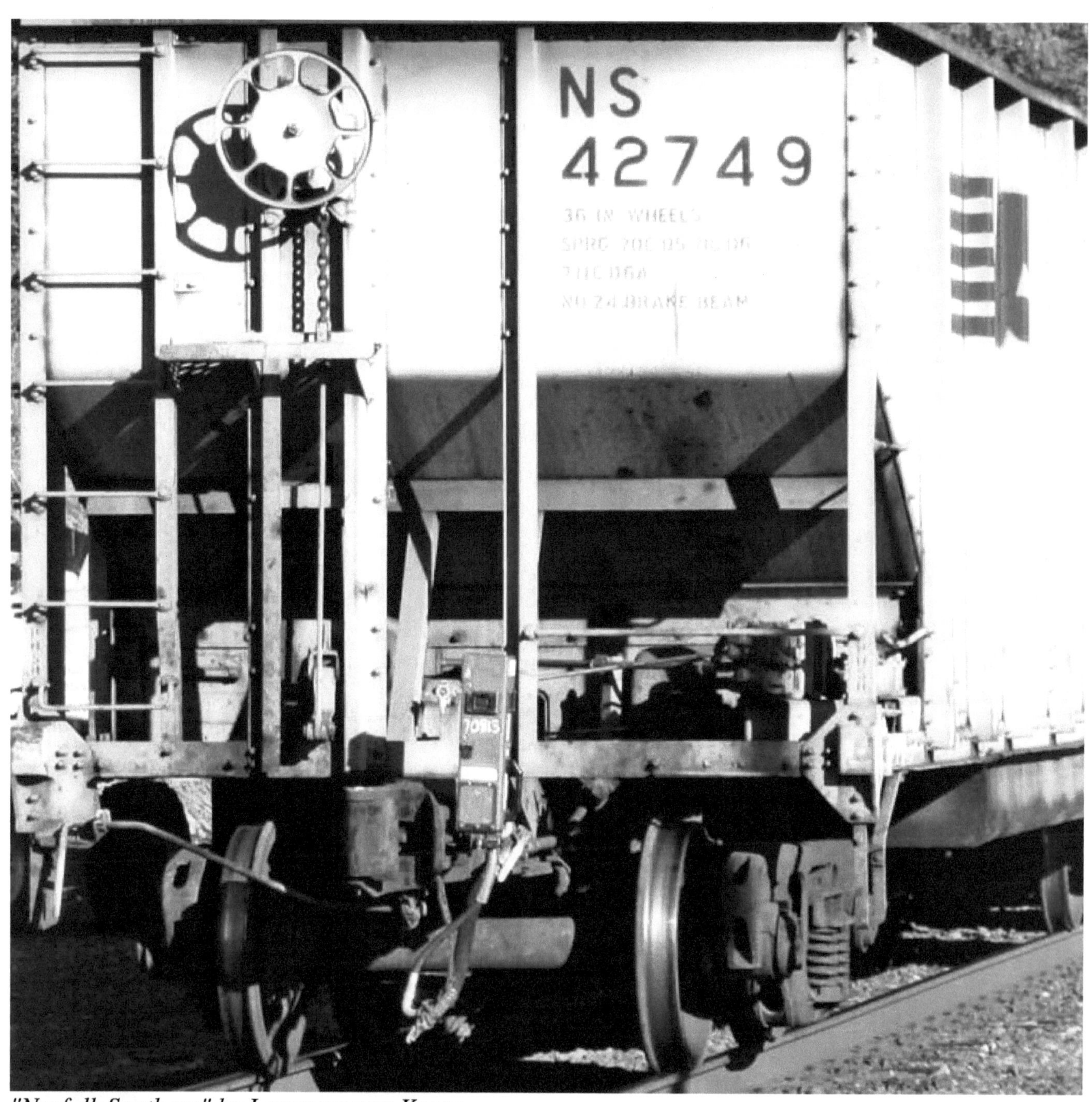

"Norfolk Southern" by Lawrence von Knorr

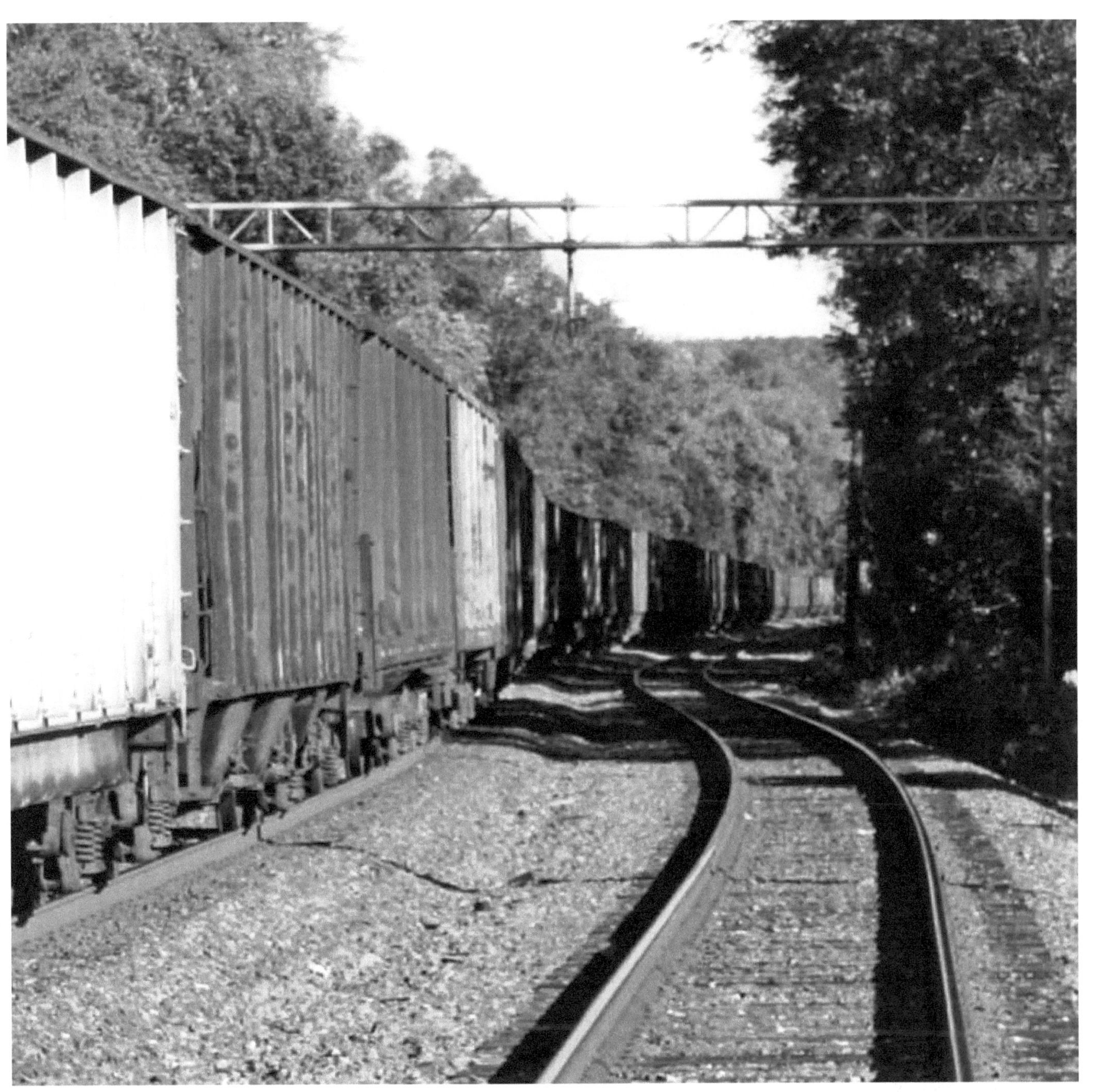

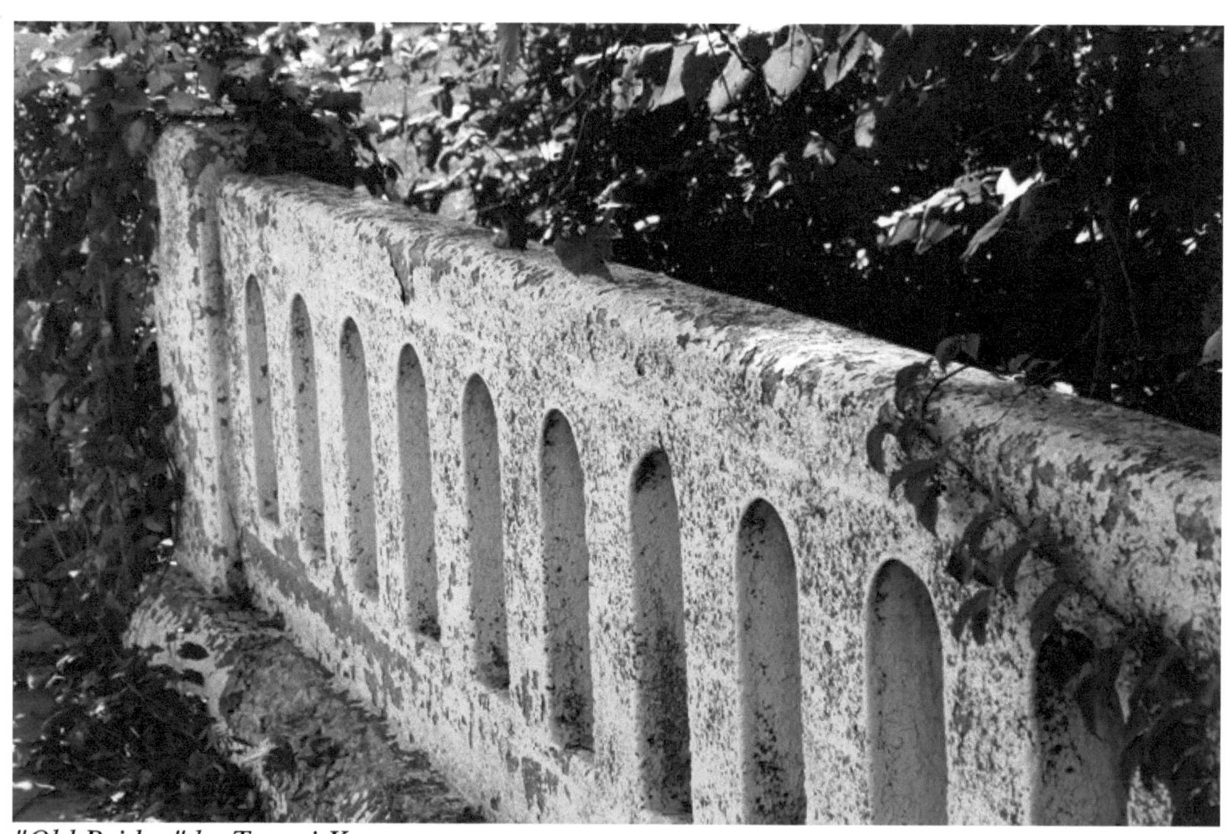
"Old Bridge" by Tammi Knorr

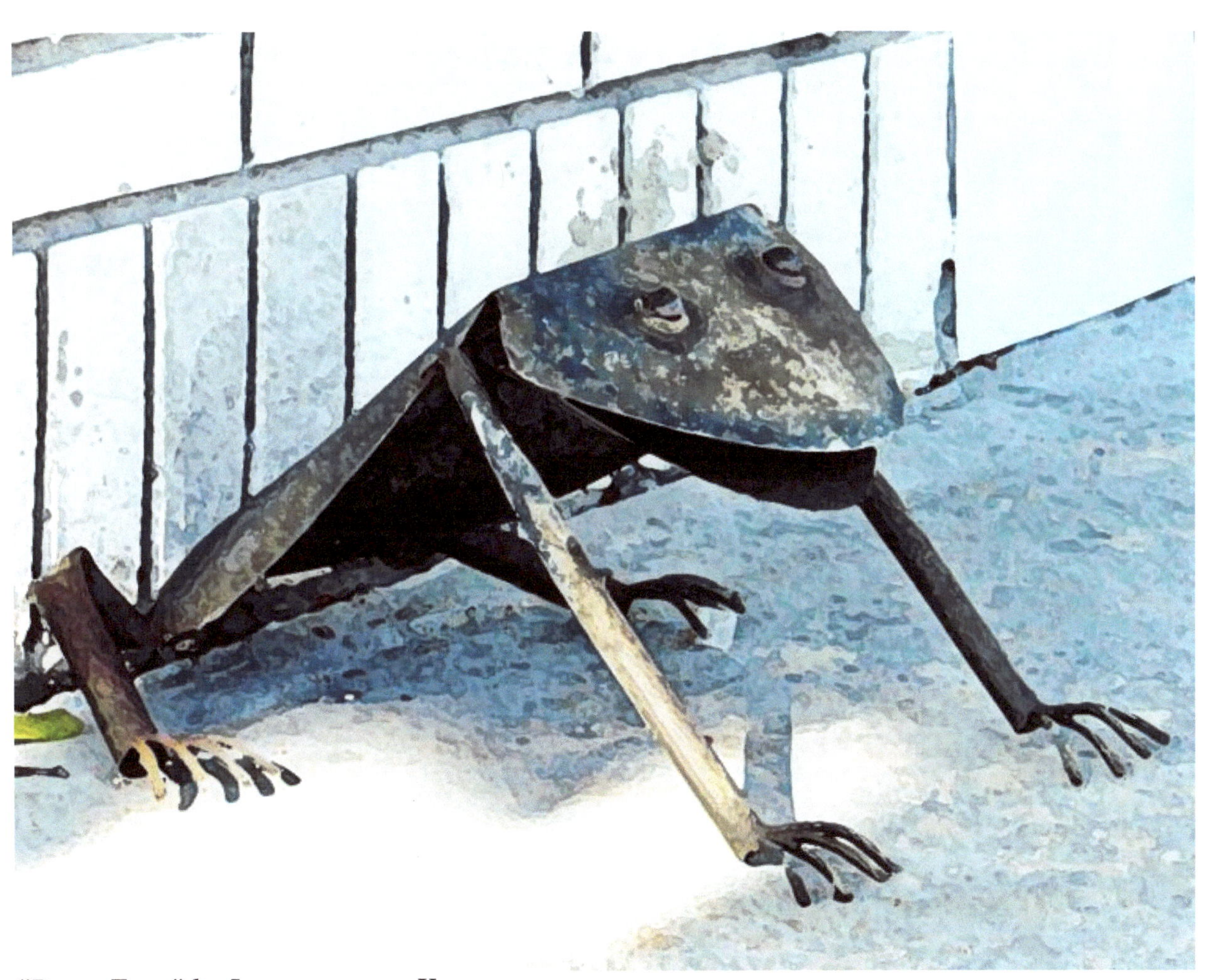

"Rusty Frog" by Lawrence von Knorr

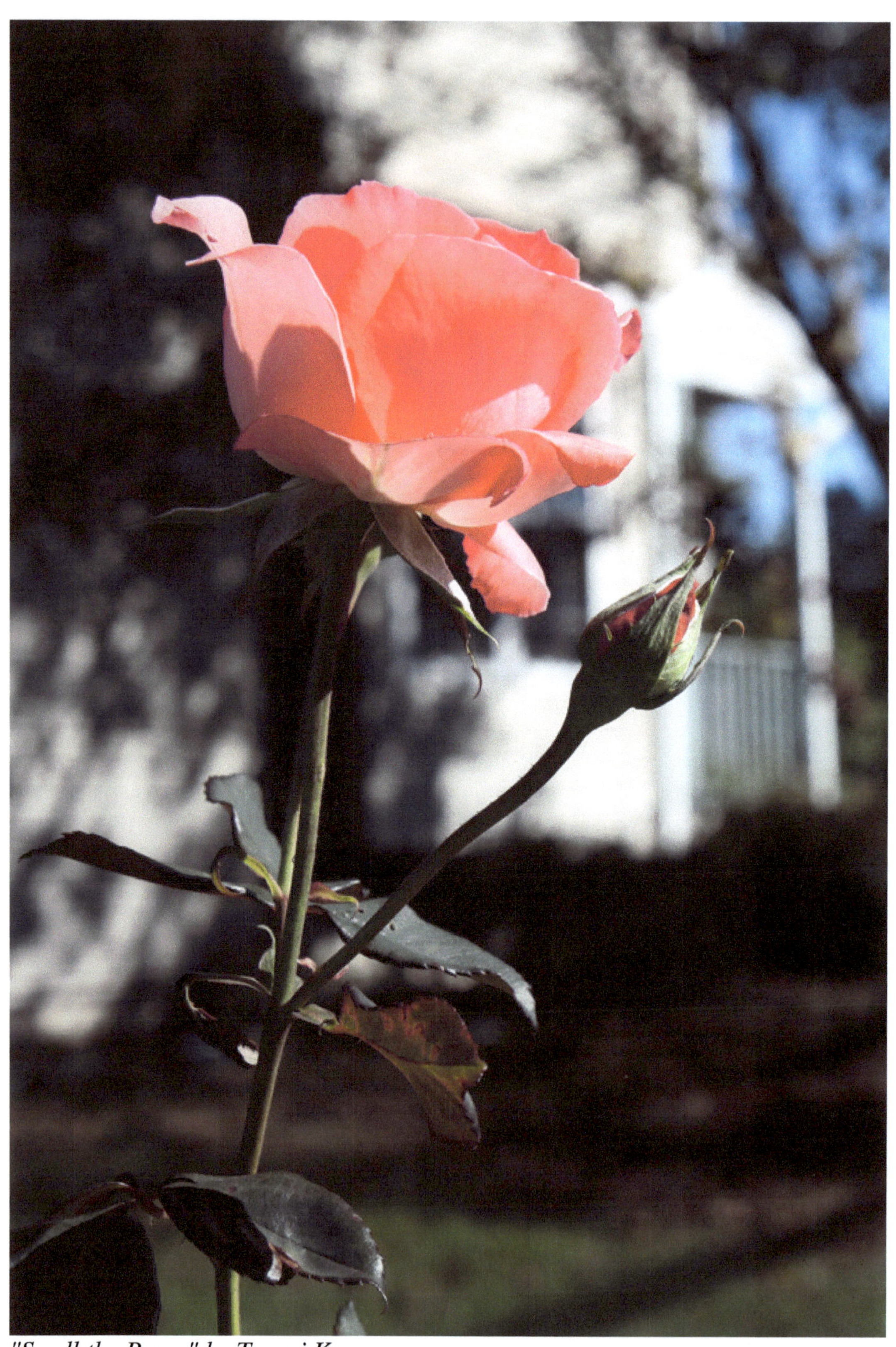

"Smell the Roses" by Tammi Knorr

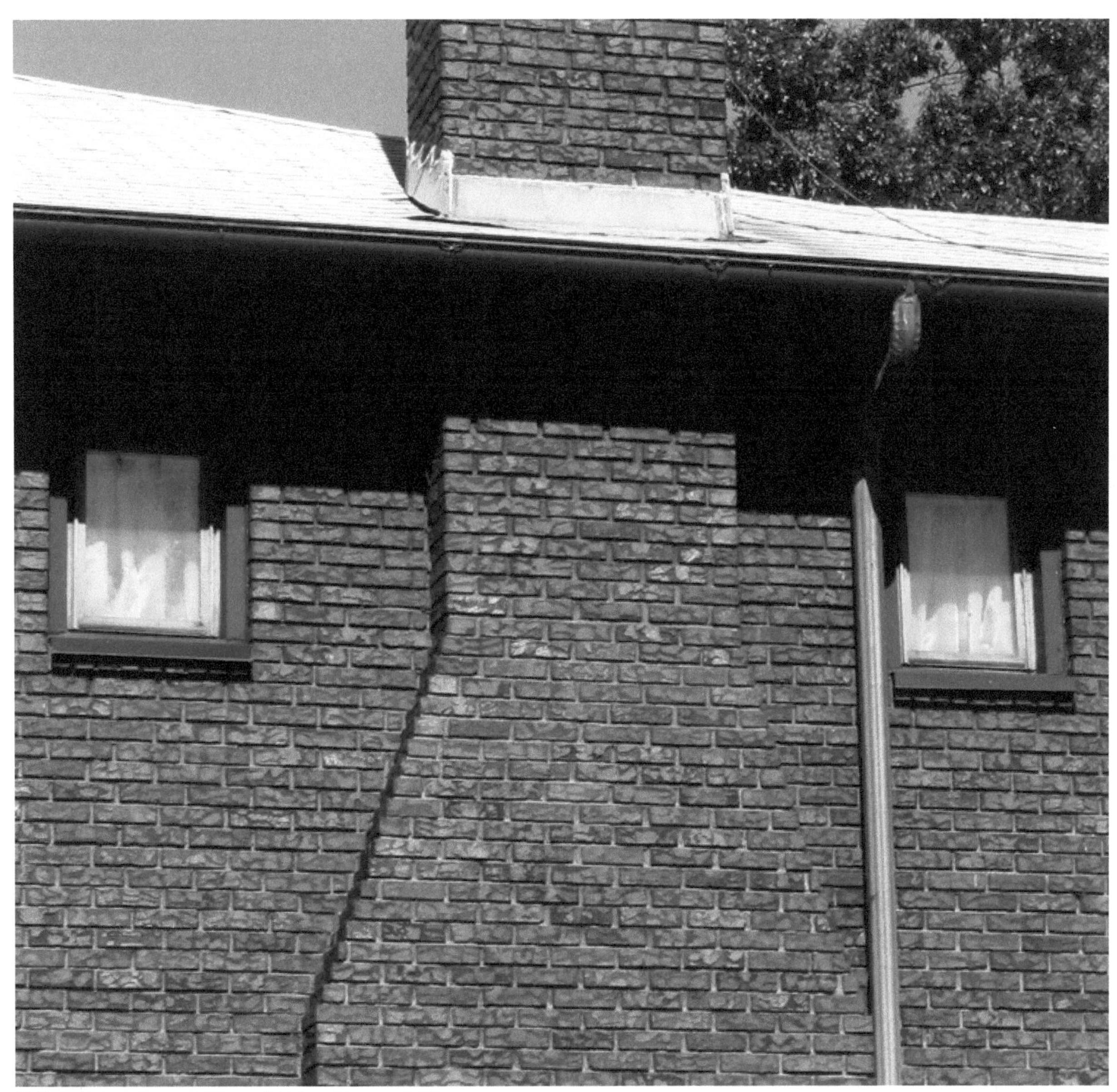

"Neighborhood Watch" by Tammi Knorr

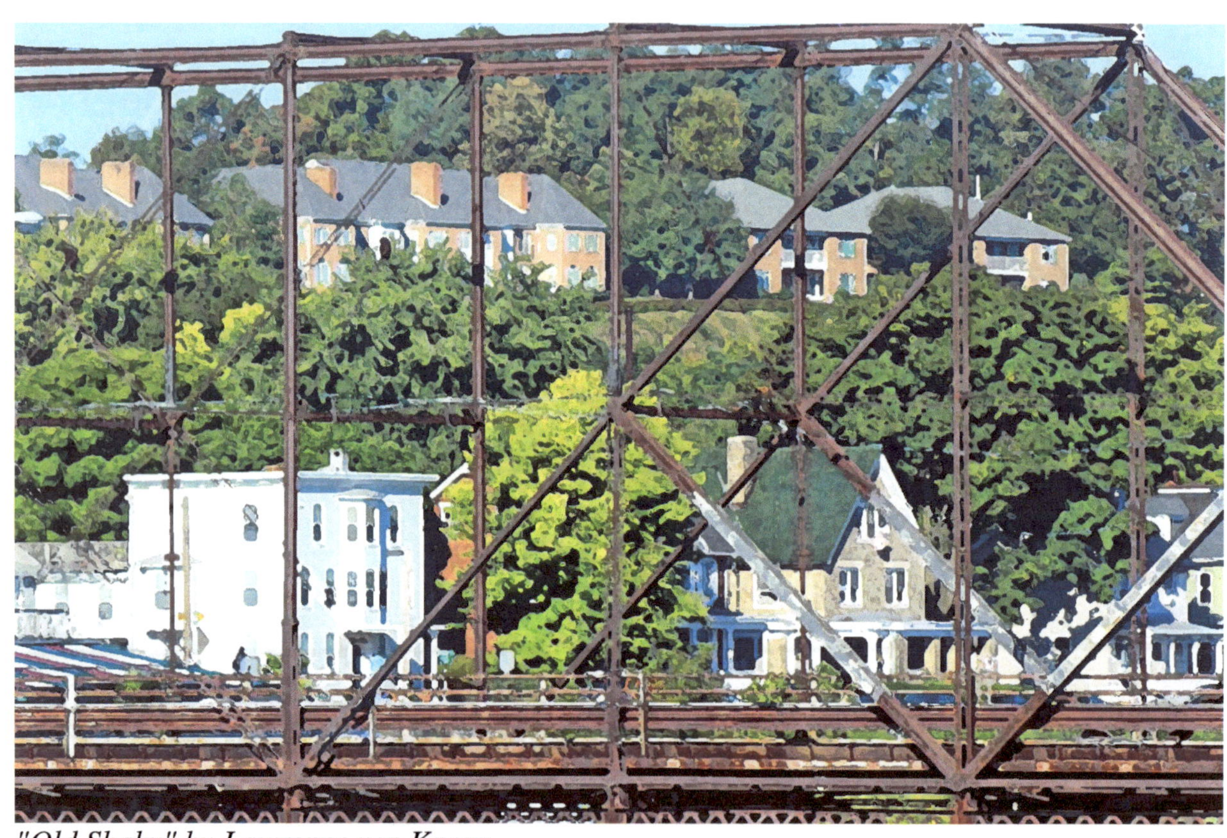

"Old Shaky" by Lawrence von Knorr

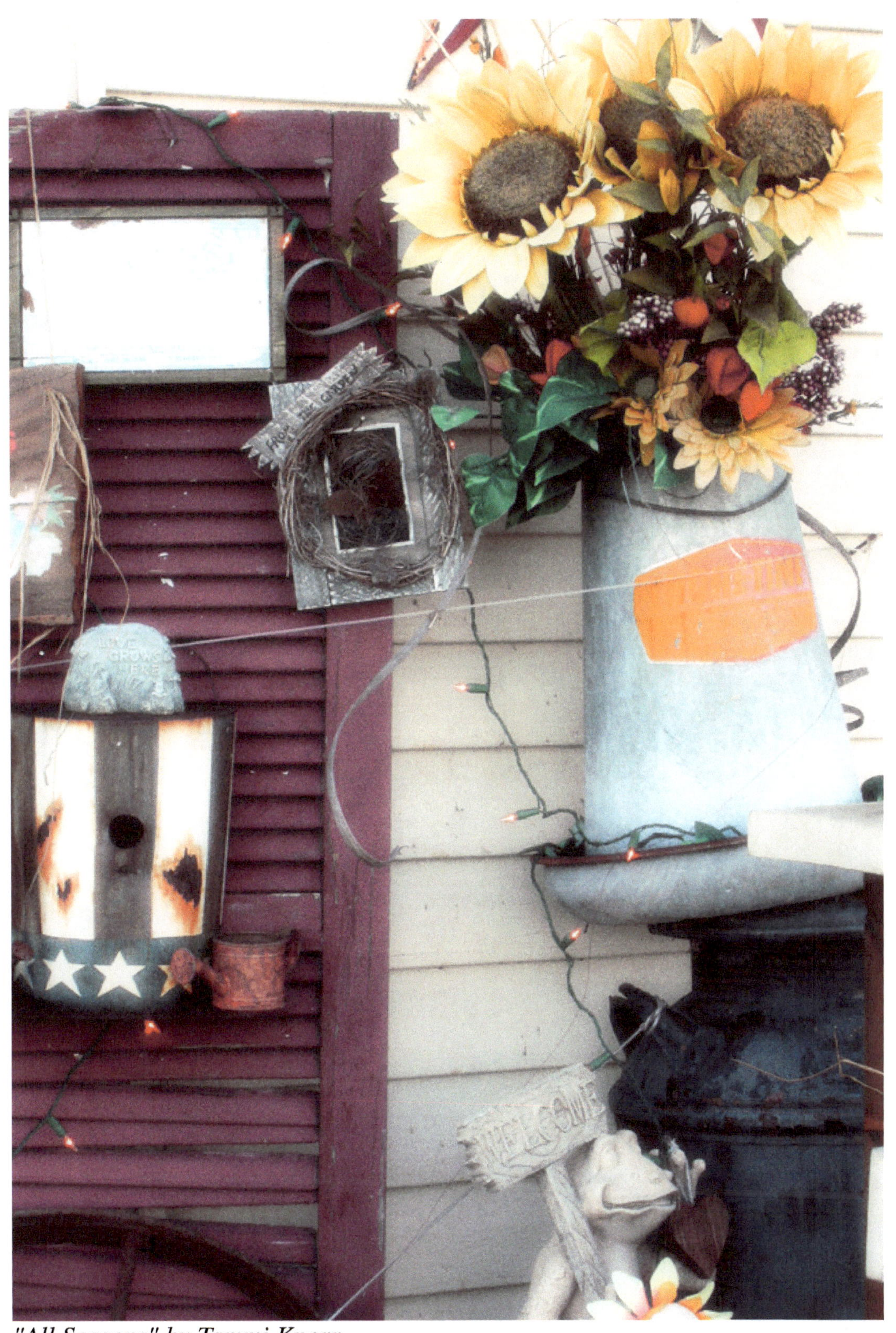

"All Seasons" by Tammi Knorr

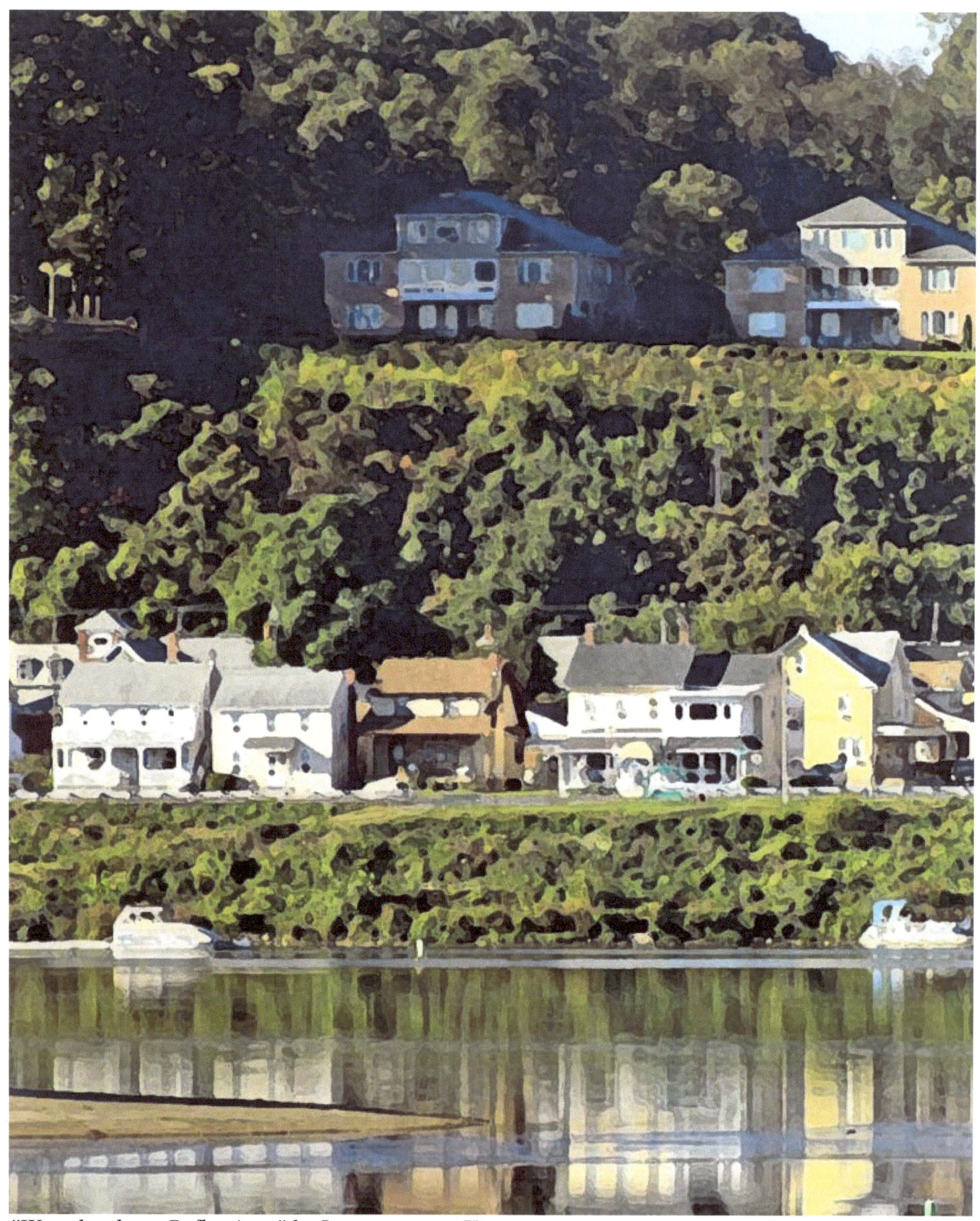

"Wormleysburg Reflections" by Lawrence von Knorr

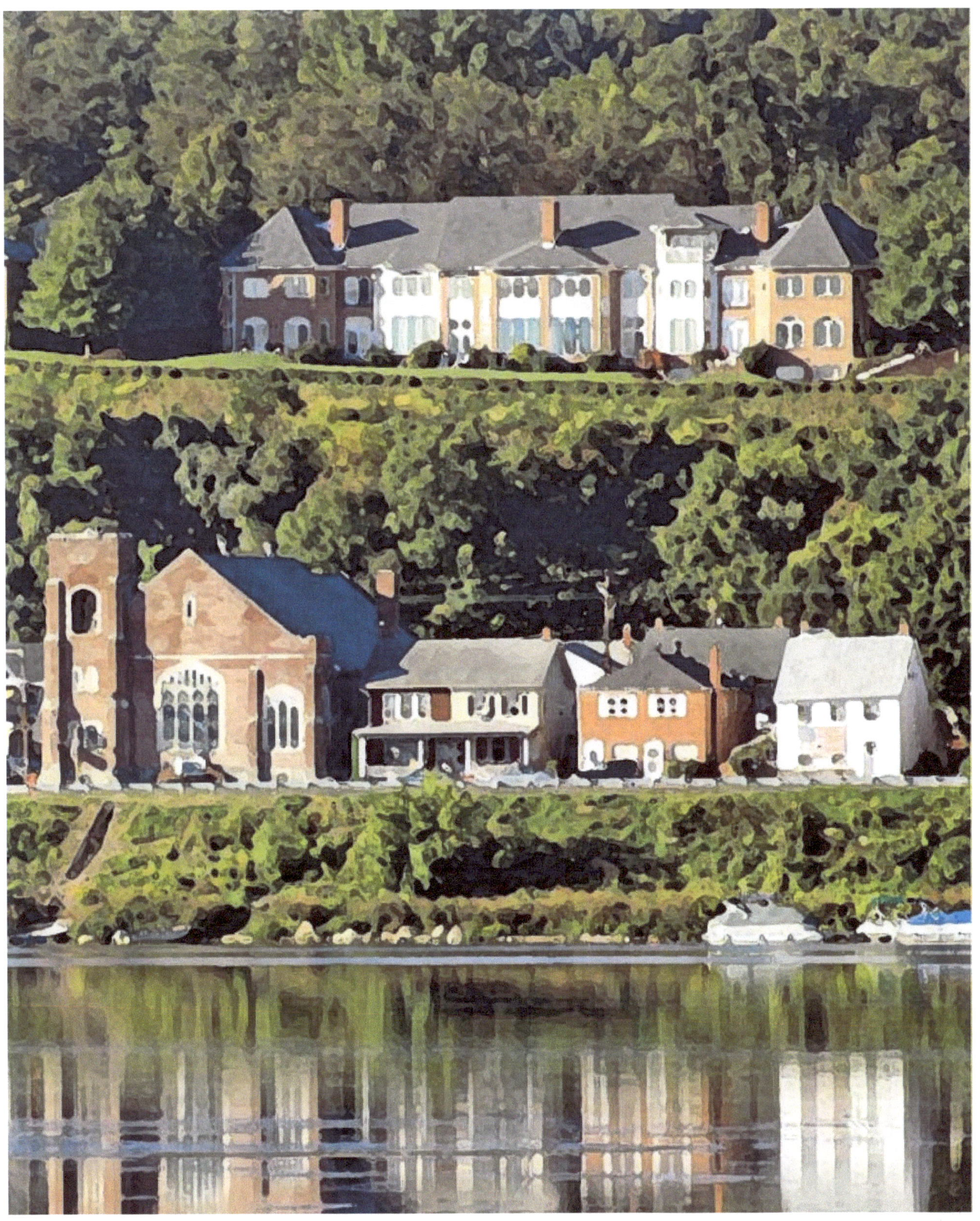

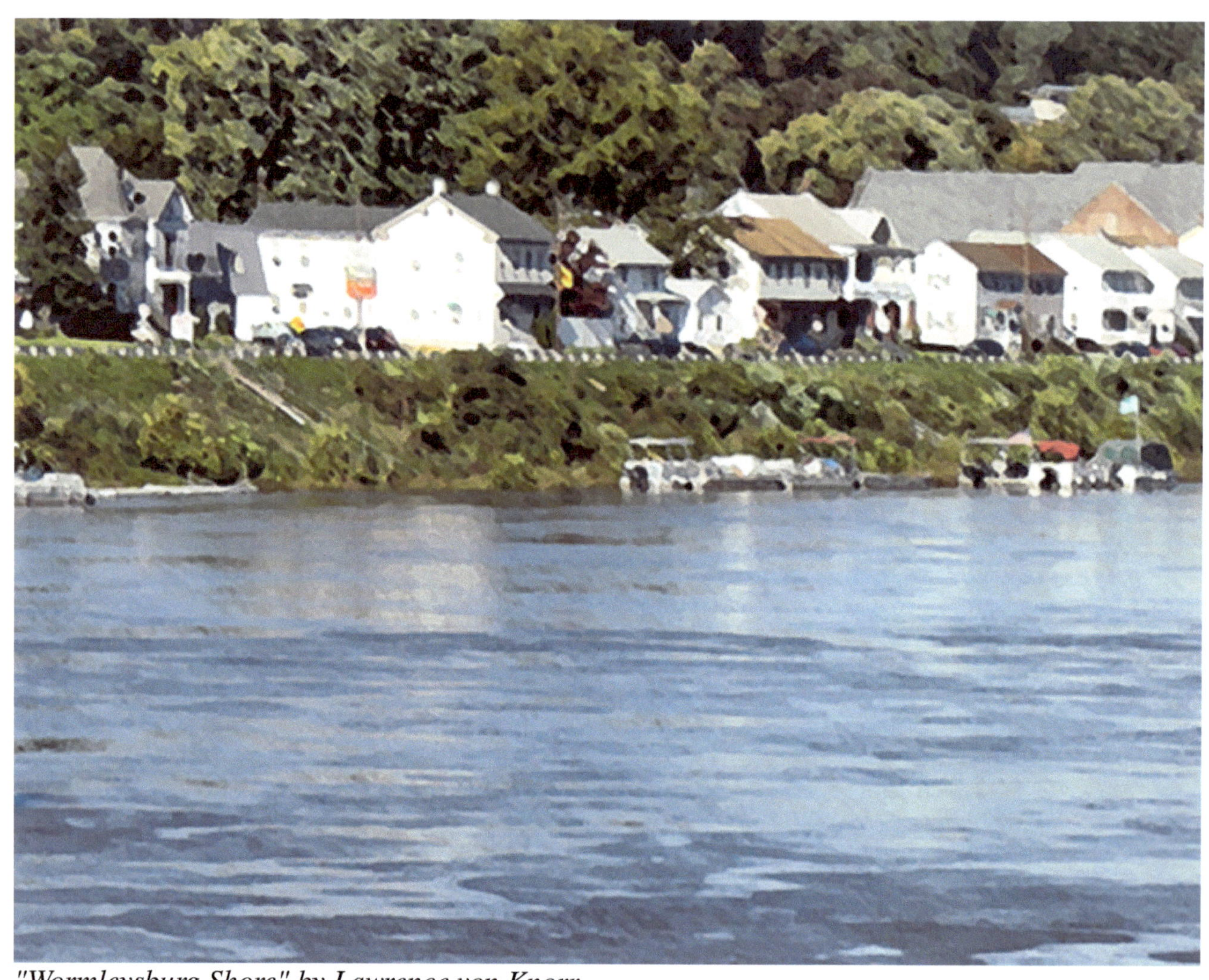

"Wormleysburg Shore" by Lawrence von Knorr

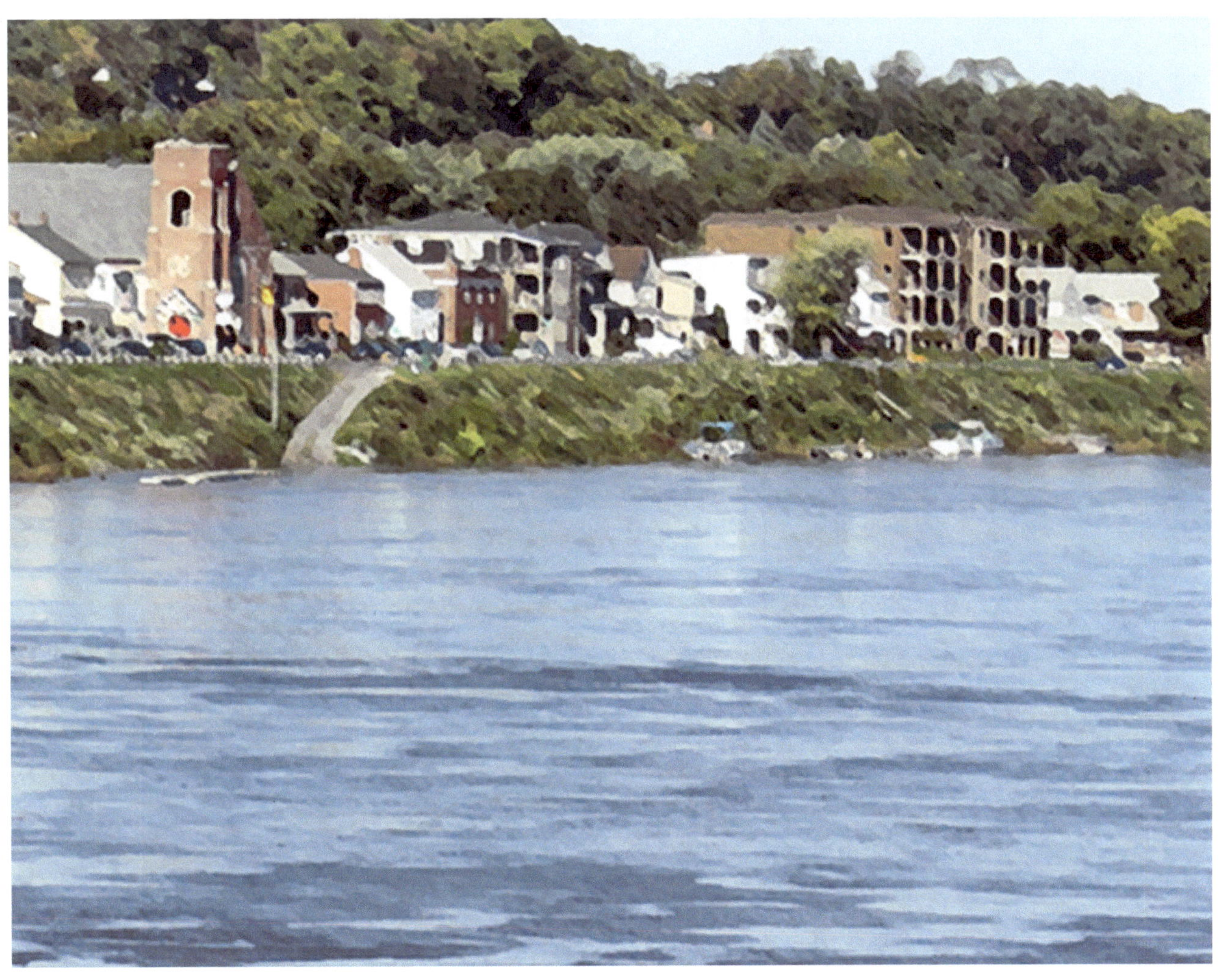

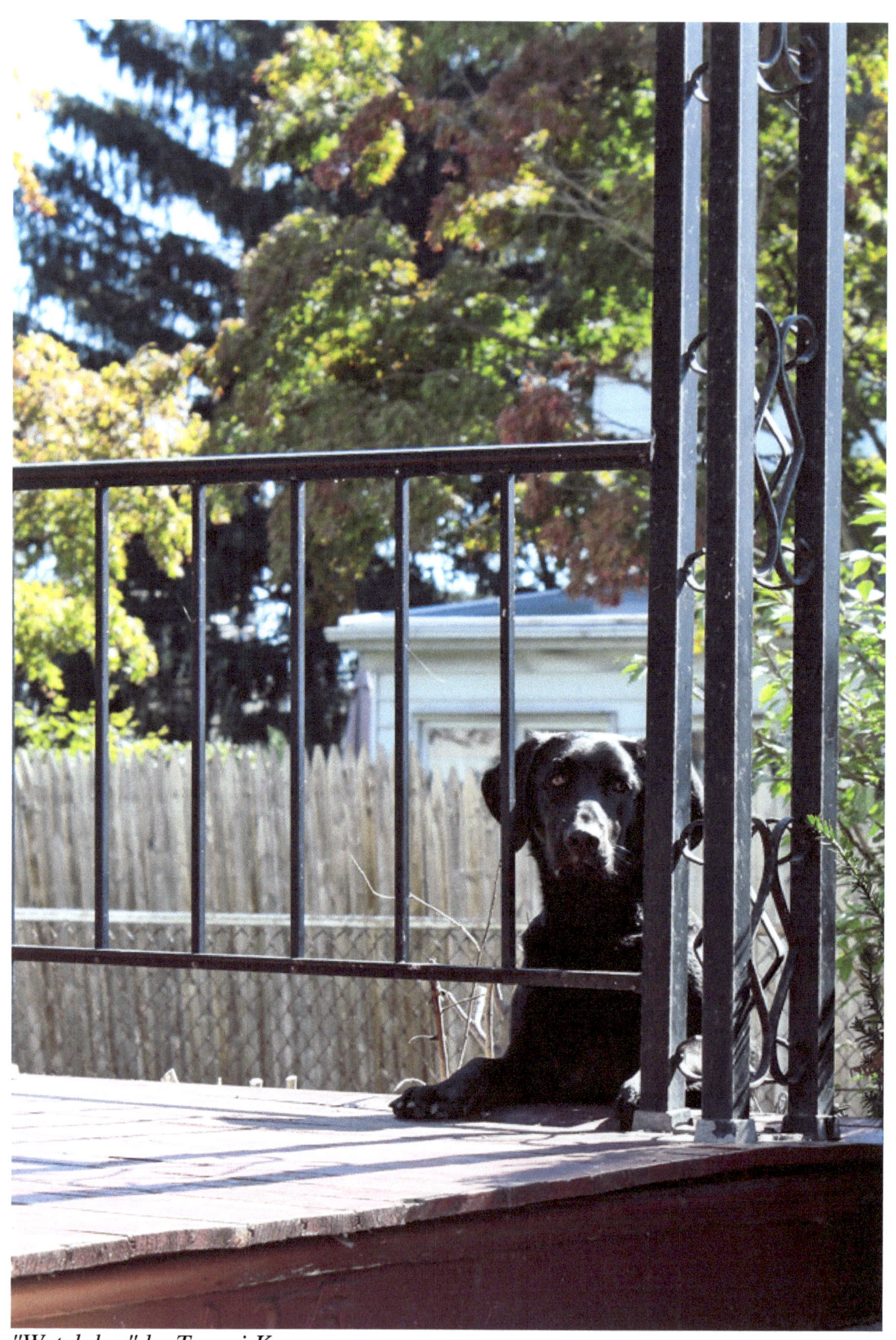

"Watchdog" by Tammi Knorr

www.ingramcontent.com/pod-product-compliance
Lightning Source LLC
LaVergne TN
LVHW070152110826
845147LV00002B/384

* 9 7 8 1 9 3 4 5 9 7 1 9 4 *